Building New Bridges

reaching and teaching children
through mid-week clubs

Building New Bridges

reaching and teaching children
through mid-week clubs

Claire Gibb

Illustrated by
Richard Warren

National Society/Church House Publishing

National Society/Church House Publishing
Church House
Great Smith Street
London
SW1P 3NZ

ISBN 0 7151 4862 1

First published in 1996 by The National Society and Church House Publishing

Illustrations by Richard Warren
Cover design by Lee Barnes, 2Q
Page design and typesetting by Church House Publishing
Printed by The Cromwell Press Ltd, Melksham, Wiltshire

Contents

Preface

For David

This book comes mainly as a result of my experience during the last six years working for local churches who considered reaching children in the locality and at present outside the church as a priority (or were willing for their employed children's worker to do so). I am therefore indebted both to St Paul's, Chipperfield, St Ebbe's, Oxford and the children of both localities for enthusiastically receiving my ideas.

Much of the material for the programme pages has come directly from ideas thrashed out during marathon termly planning meetings with teams of dedicated club leaders at St Ebbe's. I'm very grateful to them for their creative ideas and also their permission to print them and take the credit myself! Special thanks must go to Paul Dale, Ruth Froggatt and Sallie Hanlon whose positive criticisms, proof readings, encouragement and enthusiasm have been invaluable.

There are many other people too numerous to mention with whom I have worked, studied and played, who have influenced my thinking and experience over the years and so led me to this point. I am most grateful to all these people, especially my family and most of all David and Oscar – David for his daily support, patience, advice and putting up with my nose being constantly in a computer and my thoughts elsewhere; and Oscar for his constant companionship.

Then Jesus came to them and said, 'All power in heaven and on earth is given to me. So go and make followers of all people in the world. Baptise them in the name of the Father and the Son and the Holy Spirit. Teach them to obey everything I have told you. You can be sure that I will be with you always. I will continue with you until the end of the world.'

Matthew 28.18-20

PART 1

Setting up your club

CHAPTER 1

Reaching Children

Identifying the need – who are we reaching and why?

At the present time, about six out of seven children in Britain have almost no contact with the Church. This has meant that the teaching and explanation of the Christian faith to children has fallen to a worryingly low level. The General Synod Board of Education and Board of Mission responded by publishing a report in 1991 entitled *All God's Children?* (NS/CHP, 1991) which points out that the Church needs new priorities in order to communicate the gospel to the millions of children who face adult life without any awareness of a God who loves them. Above all, local churches should be challenged to take children seriously and to develop a new strategy for children's work and evangelism.

It is my belief that these children need to be reached, and need to be reached now, by every local church. Children need to be reached now for their own sake – not as candidates for the Church of the future. Children need to be reached now as a response to Jesus' command 'go and make followers of all people in the world' (Matthew 28.19) which includes all children too. Children need to be reached now and not when they are older, because 'if we choose to leave the evangelism of children until they are older, then the battle may already be lost. The hearts and minds of our children are being forcefully moulded early in life.' (*All God's Children?*, page 82)

This book is written in response to the need to win children to the Church now and suggests a practical way forward in terms of how the local church can take children seriously and develop a new strategy for children's work and evangelism.

Meeting the need – why midweek clubs?

Today, 'only 14% of children under fifteen years of age [in this country] are in a church-related activity on a typical Sunday' (*All God's Children?*, page 3). This figure is in contrast to a survey in 1955 which stated that 83% of adults over sixteen claimed to have attended Sunday school or Bible class as children.

Sunday school attendance is no longer a national custom and Sunday church-going is the exception for children and families rather than the rule. The reasons for the decline of this custom must be partly due to the general process of secularisation and de-Christianising of our whole society. As Philip Cliff says, 'it takes only two generations to de-Christianise a people' (*The Rise and Development of the Sunday School Movement in England 1780-1980*, NCEC, 1986, page 322). We are now seeing children born to the second generation of non-Sunday school parents. So the situation nationally has changed.

Instead of sitting back and expecting parents to send their children to Sunday school as a matter of course, the Church must be involved in consciously reaching out to children and their families if we want to see them become part of the Church.

The traditional Sunday school model

There are two main reasons why the Sunday school model has become inappropriate as the chief way in which we contact children and families, the first of which applies mainly to those who have no direct church connection, but the second is relevant to all children.

First, it is increasingly apparent that Sunday is not a good day for attracting non-church children and young people into a church-based activity. Sunday is often a day for the family, and is for the majority becoming the domain of sporting fixtures and other leisure pursuits.

Second, major changes have occurred in school classrooms since the 1960s because of the development in understanding how children learn. The new approach suggests that learning by discovery and learning through activity are the most effective ways a child both learns and remembers. The traditional Sunday school model of sitting and listening is not as effective in maintaining the interest of children who are experiencing very different and more varied ways of learning at school. This, combined with an enthusiasm (by many children) for television and the computer, makes many Sunday schools look uninspiring, mediocre and boring. The traditional 'school' model has become inappropriate.

Although it is true to say that in education there is now a strong move back towards traditional teaching methods for more cognitive (mental) learning, many believe that a balance of the two approaches is ideal. Different approaches are suited to different subjects. The most effective way for children to develop their understanding

about God is a combination of activity-based, discovery learning and direct teaching – the emphasis in time being upon the former. This is because becoming a disciple and learning about God is not merely a cognitive process – it involves our emotions and indeed our whole self.

A new midweek club model

Midweek clubs provide an ideal opportunity for children to 'belong' to the local church community, as well as an opportunity to learn about Jesus. Some churches have been running clubs for many years along the lines of what could be called the 'traditional club' model. This model has invariably been one in which the children spend the majority of the session pursuing varied activities such as football, snooker, games, coffee bar, etc. These activities tended to be unrelated to the five or ten minute slot of Christian teaching given at some point during the session.

There are three main problems with this approach which lead us to a new mid-week club model. First, the children can tend to think of the teaching slot as the 'price' for coming to the rest of the evening – it is the boring part to be endured so that they can then enjoy themselves doing the other activities on offer. What comes before the teaching and what follows after bears very little relation to this short burst of teaching, and so it is seen by the children to be an intrusion rather than the focal point of the evening.

Second, children learn and remember by hearing, seeing, saying and doing. The ideal is to offer the child a great variety of activities and tasks all designed to communicate the same message. Then it will be received, remembered and acted upon the more effectively. A variety of activities also means that the level of enjoyment for the children is increased – they'll see that learning about God is fun! Of course this approach means that we might have to spend more time thinking up creative games, activities and other ways of presenting our material. The aim is that the whole evening combines together to communicate and reinforce our teaching, as well as being extremely enjoyable for the children.

Third, it is very important to the development of their faith that young children have the benefit of participating in a fellowship or family of people who believe in and seek to live by the story of Jesus. This is what faith developmentalists like John Westerhoff and James Fowler call the affiliative stage of faith development. Whilst we do not want to accept the thinking of such faith developmentalists uncritically, it has provided us with some useful insights for our work with children under ten. For young children, experience of faith is very important. And for older children it is important too that they can 'belong' to a wider family or fellowship of people who believe in, and spend their lives following, Jesus. A mid-week club model centred on learning about Jesus provides children with the opportunity both to experience faith and to belong to the family of believers through learning together about Jesus with others from the church (club leaders).

There is an ongoing debate within children's and youth work concerning the material which we use in our teaching and whether it is Bible-based or topic-based (and Bible supported). This book is written using the Bible-based approach, and as it is of fundamental importance for the rest of the book, it is worth looking in some detail at the reasons why I favour this approach:

◆ God has chosen to speak to us through the Bible. Therefore our teaching material should come as a result of looking at the Bible. We should let the Bible set the agenda, rather than set the agenda ourselves.

◆ Our aim is to help children and young people to become disciples of Jesus. It is through reading, studying and learning from the Bible that we discover what being a disciple means.

◆ In working with children we should be giving them a model for how they themselves can read, study and learn about being a disciple as they grow up. This model is one in which we look to the Bible ourselves and learn from it how we should live, what God is like, why Jesus came, etc.

◆ A Bible-based approach is extremely relevant to the child's experience. God has chosen to speak to us through the Bible, and as God's words the Bible is eternally relevant. It is, however, important that we spend time applying the message from the Bible appropriately for the children. Being appropriate to the child's experience is vital in everything we do. Teaching from the Bible not only relates to the child's experience, but enables the child to relate God and His truth to their experiences, the way they live and what happens to them day by day as well.

◆ Educationally speaking, young children learn well from stories. The Bible is full of stories which we can use as they are to aid children in their understanding of the Christian faith. Of course it may be that for some children it is only the story itself which is remembered, rather than any understanding of the purpose or meaning of the story and what can be learnt from it. There are many adult disciples of Jesus (myself included) who as children were told stories from the Bible which had little meaning or significance at the time but whose significance and meaning was understood more fully later on in life. Although our ideal is to aid children's understanding, providing the framework for greater understanding in the future is important because we can never guarantee that what we have endeavoured to communicate has been understood. Opening the children to the stories from the Bible means that we are giving them the opportunity to discover their meaning and significance more fully later in life, even if they do not understand their significance at the time (as ideally we would want them to).

Summary

Sunday schools emerged from the social situation of their day – initially to provide a general education for children, and later to teach them the Christian faith. What is a suitable model for the social situation in which we find ourselves today?

For many churches, the mid-week club model has tremendous potential as far as winning the unchurched is concerned. Holiday clubs and other such special events are ideal for having a big 'burst' of outreach attracting many more children than would regularly come to Sunday services or events, and to start teaching the Christian faith. However, if our aim is for unchurched and churched children to have the opportunity to become disciples, then a more regular (weekly) and long-term means of teaching is what is needed. Weekly clubs can also be used to back up the initial interest generated by a holiday club, or other big outreach event. An integrated weekly club with the whole evening's activities centred around learning about God, (perhaps with purely 'social' events monthly or one week in three) seems to have maximum scope for reaching unchurched children. Clubs are set up to achieve what the Sunday school achieved for many children in the past – to help them learn about God in a way that is relevant and enjoyable. The long-term aim is to help them understand God's love for them (revealed supremely in the life and sacrificial death of Jesus) and to show them how to become followers of Jesus themselves if they choose to.

Such clubs can also provide many parents, both working and non-working, with a valuable service which will help to foster a more positive attitude from them towards the Church. It is possible to put on various activities as part of the club programme in order to make the most of fostering these positive links with whole families. This tie-in between outreach to children and meeting the needs of parents might well lead to a wider ministry of outreach to whole families previously unconnected with the Church. Whilst this should not be the main aim of our work with children, it can be an excellent by-product of it.

For those who at present have no contact with the Church at all, clubs may provide a valuable link with or bridge to the formal Church setting of services and meetings. It may well be that many children and young people who have been regular club attenders and so gained an understanding of the Christian faith in an informal setting might want to make the further step of coming regularly on a Sunday or to other mid-week (and more formal) meetings as appropriate. In this way, they can 'belong' more fully to the family of faith. Where children take part in Church activities, in time their parents may well wish to come along too.

"parents may wish to come along too ..."

Making a decision to take children seriously and to develop a new strategy for children's work and evangelism is a big step. As with everything, the priority is to spend time praying about every aspect of the work and every decision that is made. Reaching children is God's work and it is vital that we commit all planning meetings, discussions and decisions to Him.

The pages that follow give some practical advice on how to go about setting up a weekly club for children. I have not included advice to pray in detail for every section but rather have taken it for granted that it will be something which will constantly be the priority in our research, planning and ultimately the week-to-week running of our club. Above all, the work upon which you embark needs to be surrounded in prayer. It is in this that the key to the success of your club lies.

The following are questions to ask about your church programme and outreach to children and families. Consider the activities in your church which are already set up, e.g. Sunday programme, family services, uniformed organisations, clubs, toddler groups.

Do they attract non-Church children/young people?

If not is it because:

◆ People don't know about them?

◆ The activities are not suitable/interesting/attractive to non-Church young people or children?

◆ They are at a time or place that is inconvenient for people? (Remember that for many families it is an effort to come to any type of church event, and therefore you want to make it as easy as possible initially for them to come.)

If activities already exist but are not appropriate in some way, consider adapting them to make them more suitable.

Alternatively, consider setting up a completely new venture. The following questions might help you in deciding details of the new venture:

◆ What are the needs of your 'target' group?

◆ Is transport a problem?

◆ What age groupings make sense?

◆ Are there many single-parents and/or working parents?

◆ Are particular days or times more suitable than others?

◆ Are there other regular attractions locally attended by many children which make some days or times undesirable?

◆ What interests the children you are hoping to attract?

◆ Have they specific social or emotional needs?

It might be an idea to survey your target area to give you up-to-date information about the people who live there, their needs, problems, etc. A survey is also a good way of increasing the profile of the church within the area and preparing the way and publicising a new event to which you'd like the people to come.

CHAPTER 2

The Child's World

The children we are hoping to work with do not exist in isolation. They are part of the whole society, local community and some kind of family unit. They are therefore influenced by the society, community and family in which they live. If we want to provide a club that is relevant and appropriate for these children, it is vital that we understand the kinds of things which mould

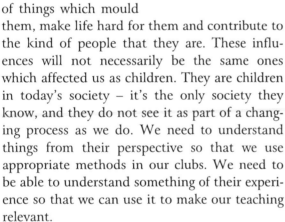

them, make life hard for them and contribute to the kind of people that they are. These influences will not necessarily be the same ones which affected us as children. They are children in today's society – it's the only society they know, and they do not see it as part of a changing process as we do. We need to understand things from their perspective so that we use appropriate methods in our clubs. We need to be able to understand something of their experience so that we can use it to make our teaching relevant.

Of course the influences will not be exactly the same for each individual child. But we can categorise the broad areas which will affect them. The categories I have used to cover the main influences are family, school, environment, media and friends. Each category includes a list of questions which you might like to ask about the children (or potential children) in your group, to help you to understand the world from their perspective.

Families

Most children have spent the majority of their life so far as part of some kind of family unit. Therefore for many children it is their family situation which has most shaped their life and will continue to do so. This is an important reason to try as a church to get to know not only children, but whole families as well. It is especially important when working with under 10s, and so including whole families should be one of our main objectives alongside reaching the children themselves. There might well be as many different family situations as there are children in your club – here are a few of the main ones:

Two-income families – both parents working outside the home. Children can sometimes be neglected in terms of attention.

Cohabiting families – more and more people live together outside marriage. The children might be from that relationship or from a previous relationship or marriage. Children who live in such families may find commitment hard to understand.

Extended families – because of divorce, abuse or financial hardship children are brought up by others in the family or outside the family instead of their real parents. Also families from other cultures and religions live in extended families, with perhaps several generations and cousins living under the same roof.

Single-parent families – often part of the stress for children with one parent looking after them is financial hardship.

Step-families – about three out of four divorced people remarry. Adjusting to living in a step family is often difficult for children, and adjusting to the sense of loss suffered from 'losing' one parent or feelings of not being accepted by the new partner can make the child insecure.

One-income two-parent families – this category is becoming increasingly small in comparison with the others.

What sort of families do the children in your group come from?

Of course even taking into account the specific circumstances above does not give us all the information we need about a child's family experience. There are other factors which vary over the whole range of family set-ups such as:

◆ How are their needs met at home – physical, emotional, mental, spiritual?

◆ How are they valued, or are they just treated as an inconvenience?

◆ How is education valued ?

◆ How do they spend time together as a family? Or do they hardly ever see each other?

◆ What is the financial situation at home?

◆ How are they disciplined?

◆ How are they given responsibility? Is it appropriate for their age?

School

After the home environment one of the other major forces which shapes a child is the school environment. Children attend day schools thirty-nine weeks a year for six and a half hours a day. This means that about a third of their waking time is spent at school. The ethos of the school, methods of teaching employed, discipline policy, content of the lessons and influence of the teachers all affect children's attitudes to life. These things will not only shape the children you work with, but will have a knock-on effect for your club programme. If the school is one where what the

children have to say is treated with interest and respect, then you are more likely to have good discussions and questions during the presentation of your Bible material. If children are given the impression at school that it's more important to sit and listen, then they will find it harder to enter into discussion, put forward their own point of view and to think through the issues with which you are presenting them. Obviously the discipline policy the children are used to, as well as the content of their learning and the teaching methods the schools employ, will all affect your work. You might also find that what they are being taught at school is in conflict with what you are teaching them. This situation needs to be handled with sensitivity, and it is important to remember that 'a school within the state education system cannot be a community committed to the truth of the gospel in the sense that a local church-based children's activity would be' (*All God's Children?* page 24). Schools within the state education system are committed to a multi-cultural policy which will usually mean the teaching of many faiths. Any teaching which is done, is framed in terms of belief and not fact. Thus Christianity is not handled in the same way as science or geography in terms of factual knowledge. But fact as well as faith is involved when we speak of Jesus.

Find out what kind of schools your children attend. If possible visit them, and perhaps try to build up good relationships with the staff. Many primary schools are open to well trained, prepared people coming in to take assemblies – you can use this and other opportunities to work alongside the schools in your area. A good link between the church and school is of great advantage to the work you will do.

Ask these questions of the school(s) which your children attend:

◆ What is the the ethos of the school?

◆ What methods of teaching are employed?

◆ What is the discipline policy?

◆ What is the content of the lessons? Is there a particular emphasis or specialism in the school?

◆ How is religious education handled in the school?

Environment

As well as the home and school environment, the child's wider environment will also have an influence on him or her. Issues such as the housing the child lives in will affect how keen (s)he is to do certain activities at club. Children who do not have an opportunity to run around a lot at home or 'let off steam' after school and before coming to the club will probably value lively active games. The home and area environment might restrict what the child can do in his or her free time, and therefore influence what you decide to do at the club. The answers to the questions below might direct the type of programme you offer the children, and so might be useful to think through:

◆ What kind of housing do the children live in – estates, high-rise flats, terraces, etc?

◆ What kind of area do the children live in – suburbia, rural, inner-city?

◆ Does the area have a good number of amenities?

◆ Are there other types of provision made for the children by the community – youth clubs, brownies, holiday community projects, etc?

◆ What about transport – is there good public transport, or is it an area mainly of car-owners?

Media

Television occupies more time than any other media in history. In many if not most families, television consumes the majority of the available time for a family to be together. Many children have televisions in their own rooms and Britain has the highest ownership of video cassette recorders in proportion to its population in the world. There are many positive aspects of television viewing:

◆ Television widens children's horizons, and gives them a more worldwide view of humanity.

◆ Television is educational and so knowledge and understanding are improved.

◆ Leisure and sport are given a high profile on television and so children can be encouraged to participate in various activities which they might not otherwise engage in.

◆ Some television presentations can encourage a wider perspective as far as poverty and need in other countries of the world are concerned, and can persuade children to be more actively involved in helping raise money, etc.

But there are also negative aspects of television viewing which can and do shape children's lives to their detriment.

◆ The open door: in *Children at Risk,* David Porter argues that 'television is an open door. It brings to the home the cinema and the rock concert, the sports field and the stage. Some of these are not at all suitable for children.' (*Children at Risk*, Kingsway, 1986, page 39). Report after report tells us that children watch long hours of television daily, including hours supposedly reserved for adult viewing. Unless viewing is monitored by responsible adults, it brings the child into contact with all kinds of programmes which are both inappropriate and harmful. Even if these programmes do not seem to be harmful at the time (an effect which is difficult to measure in any case) there are profound implications for what it is teaching as 'acceptable' and 'normal' behaviour and the way television is subtly undermining the values of society.

◆ Visual reality: television is a visual medium and therefore does not easily portray realities which are not visual in nature. Because of the emphasis on the visual nature of everything, 'good' television is nearly always action-packed, fast-moving, providing situations which are constantly changing and programmes which are slickly presented. These features combine to present children with an imbalanced view of life and inappropriate expectations of what the 'real' world is like.

◆ Disappearing childhood: in *The Disappearance of Childhood*, (Laurel Books, 1982) Neil Postman argues that television has made the controlling of information impossible, and thus childhood has started to disappear. 'Everything which previously maintained childhood is altered – the kind of information to which the child has access, its quality, sequence, and the circumstances in which it is experienced. Without secrets there is no childhood. And television cannot keep secrets of any kind.' (*Children and God*, Ron Buckland, SU, 1988, page 111). Whilst there are obvious advantages to children having access to more information about a variety of issues, the maintenance of childhood depends to some extent upon managed information and sequential learning. A child has no framework of experience, emotion or understanding in which to put randomly inundated information intended for adults. There is a vast difference between a child's ability to understand and sort pieces of information and an adult's ability to do the same. Children might soon become overloaded with inappropriate information, and then may lose all sense of curiosity and wonder. We need to control the flow of information and knowledge available to the child for his or her own good.

◆ Commercial targeting: advertisements for children's toys and games for Christmas on television begins around October, and they become increasingly frequent and hard-selling leading up to Christmas itself. The media machine is a well-oiled, efficient model which sets fashions and tells children what toys to buy, games to play, clothes to wear, food to eat and music to listen to.

Answers to the following questions will give you some idea of how much the children you are working with might be influenced by television viewing.

◆ Does the child's family have a television – and video? Is there one in their own room? Are they allowed to regulate their own viewing?

◆ How much television do they watch on their own? as a family?

Friends

During teenage years peer group pressure for most children is more powerful than any other single influence. This is less true for children in the under ten age group, although it is still a significant influence. Children like to be seen to be buying, playing, wearing, eating and listening to the 'right' things by their peers, and can be ridiculed and ostracised if they do not.

Children tend to make friends more readily with others of similar attitudes and backgrounds. If going to a church-based event is considered weak or 'wet' by a child's friends, then it is difficult for that child to go 'against the flow' and carry on attending enthusiastically. A large part of children's behaviour is learned from peers either at school or at play. Peer pressure can of course work for the church's benefit. If the clubs you are setting up are seen by groups of children as the 'in' place to be, then you might well be inundated with enthusiastic young people longing to take part!

Children are more likely to have this view of clubs if they are fun, enjoyable, relevant and if their programmes and leaders show a good understanding of the child's world.

CHAPTER 3
The Children Act

The Children Act 1989, a significant reform of legislation relating to children, has major implications for all those working with children, including churches. It is designed to encourage good practice and safety and three of the key principles behind it are:

◆ The welfare of the child comes first

◆ Shared responsibility for the child

◆ Co-operation not confrontation

Although there are many ways in which the Act might be relevant to the work of the Church, the section of most relevance (both to most churches and to this book) is that of work with the under eights.

This section states that organisations which run an activity for under eights which lasts two hours or more, and for more than six days a year are required to register the activity with the local authority. As most after-school or mid-week clubs will not run for as long as two hours a week (excluding preparation and tidying up time) then it is unlikely that you will need to register your club. However, as the Act is concerned with good practice and the welfare of the children in our care, it may well be that we will want to follow its advice and recommendations concerning working with the under eights even though we are not obliged to. The section that follows gives the guidelines that one would have to follow if registering an activity (and can therefore be regarded as optional for those not registering), and as such is considered good practice as regards any type of work with under eights. The *Safe from Harm* Home Office

report, as well as denominational or diocesan guidelines, are worth looking at for extra information (for details see the entry for chapter 3 in the bibliography).

The persons offering care or working with children

◆ Workers should be over eighteen years of age (for insurance purposes, and to qualify in terms of the adult/child ratio. It is however possible to have extra help from responsible young people aged under eighteen with super-vision.)

◆ Workers must not have been convicted of any type of offence (especially those against children) and must sign a declaration saying so: a sample form of declaration is given at the end of this section.

◆ In particular, workers must be aware that no physical force or contact may be used when disciplining children. Great care also needs to be taken over any physical contact with children, especially by male leaders.

◆ They should be able to provide warm and consistent care.

◆ They should be committed to treating all children as equal and with equal concern.

◆ They should have good physical and mental health, integrity and flexibility.

◆ They should have training in a relevant field (or be given such).

- They should have some experience of working with children (although this need not apply to all leaders if working with a team).

- The church should take out adequate insurance to cover leaders and children during both on-site and off-site sessions (most dioceses offer insurance schemes which provide full cover).

- Insurance should cover transport to and from outside locations if you are intending to run off-site activities.

- All drivers should be experienced (and minibus drivers usually need to be over 25 too).

The suitability and safety of the premises

The premises and equipment should be maintained in a safe condition – things to consider here are:

- Availability of First Aid at all times (both personnel and kit, meaning that at least one leader on site should have sufficient knowledge in First Aid procedures).

- Accidents should be recorded and parents notified after the session.

- Availability of toilets on site.

- Up-to-date fire notices, appliances and knowledge of procedures in case of fire.

- Checking all rooms where the children will be before the club session for hazards, such as stacks of chairs small children can get under and which might fall.

- Checking all entrances and exits, so that a child cannot slip out or a stranger slip in unnoticed.

- The maximum number of people allowed on the premises is not exceeded at any time.

- Checking that all activities to be undertaken in the evening's session do not provide undue risk for the children or leaders.

The children and their care

- Parental consent and health forms should be filled in by the parent/guardian for all those children wishing to attend (even on an irregular basis). A sample form is given at the end of this section.

- An attendance register should be kept every week.

- Adult/child ratios should be suitable for both the group and the particular activity. For children under seven this should be two adults for up to eight children, and one additional adult for every eight extra children. For children aged seven upwards it is two adults for up to eight children and one additional adult for every twelve extra children. This is for 'ordinary' circumstances. Swimming baths require one adult in the water for every three children under the age of eight. For other specialist activities, you must check before you go.

Parental consent form

I give my permission for . . . . (name)
to be involved in the activities organised by the 4 to 6s club of . . . .
Church, which take place between 5.00 and 6.15pm on a Tuesday.

I understand that this will include both on- and off-site activities, and transport to and from
activities by car or minibus. I understand that all the activities will be properly supervised by adults
18 and over, and that authorised youth leaders will ensure that my child is properly looked after
at all times.

I give my permission for the youth leaders to act on my behalf as a parent, e.g. in a medical emer-
gency (this will only be used if the leaders cannot contact you).

BLOCK CAPITALS PLEASE

Parent's name . . . .

Address . . . .

. . . .

. . . .   Date of Birth . . . / . . ./ . . .

Does the child have any medical conditions we should know about? . . . .

. . . .

Signature of Parent / Guardian . . . .

Telephone number . . . .

Other contact . . . . Telephone number . . . .

Children and youth group leader's appointment form

In view of the Children Act 1989, churches are advised to ask all children and youth group leaders to complete this form. We know that all who work with children and young people would wish to ensure the best possible care for their safety and protection, and completing this form will help us greatly in this task. (Please return this form directly to the person who gave it to you. This form is confidential and we guarantee that personal details will be kept confidential by the church.)

Name . . . .

Address . . . .

. . . .

Telephone number . . . . (daytime)

. . . . (evening)

Please could you tell us something about your interests, skills and experience (if any) with

children/young people . . . .

. . . .

Have you had any relevant training? . . . .

. . . .

"I have never been convicted of a sexual offence, or an offence against children/young people."

Signed. . . . . Date . . . .

(The following only to be completed if the prospective leader is not known well by the church)

Please give us the name and address of two people who know you well (for about two years) and can provide us with a reference.

1 . . . .   2 . . . .

. . . .

. . . .

. . . .

CHAPTER 4
Starting Off

Finance

Running an effective children's programme can be an expensive business. So approaches should be made to the appropriate sources (PCCs, trust funds, etc.) well before the club gets underway. Budgeting is more difficult at first, so a good plan is to ask for a pool of money initially until you have more idea of what it is all going to cost and can plan a realistic budget. Here are a few hints for saving money:

- ◆ If finance is a real problem, children could be charged anything from a nominal amount (10p or 20p each) to your full expenses per child. However, there are big disadvantages with this – some would not agree with a philosophy of people paying to hear the Christian faith explained, and the whole thing becomes far less of a 'service' for families as well as potentially excluding some on financial grounds.

- ◆ Encourage children to meet the cost of off-site activities, except where it will prevent children from attending if they must pay.

- ◆ Build up as much free resource material as you can from various sources – scrap paper, old jam jars, empty yoghurt pots and such like.

- ◆ Look into obtaining a grant from the social services or other agencies who might give them if you are providing a free service open to any child.

- ◆ Put on fun fund-raising activities to get it started – children can be involved in this too, and it increases the profile of the venture.

Finding a team

Quality leadership is the key to successful children's ministry. Finding a suitable group of other people who are willing to be part of a team setting up the new venture is crucial. The earlier the team is set up the better – it is good to discuss and brainstorm everyone's ideas even at the planning stage, before questions of day, time, age-group, etc. are decided. If the team can be involved in the survey (either formal or informal) of your target area which you have undertaken at an earlier stage, it provides a really good opportunity for the team to get to know each other, the area, and also perhaps build contacts with people in the area very early on. Having a good look at what's going on already is useful for giving ideas, seeing opportunities, and catching enthusiasm for children's outreach. The following section gives a few guidelines and hints on getting a team together.

Choosing or accepting volunteers?

"the kind of people we should be looking for"

Despite leadership being one of the crucial things which makes children's work successful, the reality for most churches and youth organisations is that recruiting leaders is one of their greatest difficulties.

The first priority when advertising for potential team members is to have thought through what type of commitment you are asking for. Do you want all the leaders to be committed to helping every week? Or are you happy to have a small core of regulars, and then other leaders who are on a rota, say coming once a month? It is important to have at least a core group of regular leaders because young children benefit greatly in terms of security and building good relationships when the same people are working with them every week. On the other hand, a few leaders on a rota might be an advantage in that it provides a good variety and also means that adults with less time available can be involved.

What about preparation before, and clearing up after the club? Will you expect all leaders to be involved in this as well?

What about planning meetings – how often, and who has to come? How often are you intending to have training sessions?

If possible, you need to have clear in your own mind the answers to these questions. You might be able to encourage one or two people with a lot of time on their hands to commit themselves in a more open-ended way, but on the whole you'll get more people volunteering if they know exactly what type of time commitment is involved. It also saves people volunteering and then having to pull out at a later date because they hadn't realised how much time it would take up.

Once you have made it clear what level of commitment you are asking of your potential team members, how do you choose the right people to work alongside you? Do you accept anyone who volunteers, realising that somebody is better than nobody? Do you accept people who have had no experience with children, or people who have no faith in Christ themselves but perhaps who love children? Or does the launch of your club wait until you've found the ideal team of gifted children's workers?

This dilemma between hand-picking or choosing a team and accepting anyone who volunteers needs handling sensitively. In practice, probably a combination of choosing individuals and accepting volunteers will result. But there are various guidelines which can help in identifying the kind of people you should be looking for to make up a good team.

First, although it is unlikely that you will need to register your club in accordance with The Children Act, its recommendations for choosing adults to work with children are certainly worth bearing in mind. The previous section deals with this issue in greater depth (see pages 12-13).

Second, the Bible provides us with a number of passages in the New Testament outlining the qualifications for those who want to serve, lead or teach others in the Church family. These are full of practical advice about the kind of people you should be looking for in the team. From these passages, they should:

◆ Read the Scriptures themselves (2 Timothy 3.15-17). The main purpose of these clubs is to teach children about Jesus and also to provide a place of Christian nurture for children. It is therefore inappropriate to have leaders who are not themselves Christians involved in teaching the children or answering their questions about faith in Christ. At the same time, it is good to recognise that not only may such leaders have a lot of skills and expertise to offer, but they might gain a lot themselves from hearing the Christian faith explained simply and clearly to the children. I have often had people who are not sure of their faith, or perhaps don't know what faith in Christ is all about, as part of a team, but with a very specific role – for instance being involved in the craft activities, running games, handling publicity, administration or other practical tasks. For their own sake and for the children's sake it is important that they are not put in a situation which involves Christian teaching.

"to try new skills"

- Be an example in the way they live (1 Timothy 4.12, 16).

- Be able to teach others in the faith (2 Timothy 4.2).

- Be willing to learn and be taught themselves. This is more important than an individual necessarily having experience with children: look for people who are open for God to continue to teach them through the Bible and use them in whatever situation they find themselves (2 Timothy 3.14-15). Like all Christians they need to be willing to learn new skills, listen to advice, respect leaders, work hard and to be extremely patient (1 Thessalonians 5.12-15).

- Have different gifts, and use them (1 Corinthians 12.4-7). Here, balance is important. If possible, have a team made up of individuals displaying a variety of gifts – avoid the tendency to think that everyone will necessarily be involved in up-front teaching, leading the singing, thinking of zany and appropriate games or craft activities. Of course at the outset it might be unclear what each individual's gifts are. As well as training, we should give each leader the opportunity to have a go at different tasks (being prepared for some to be more successful than others – a team should be a safe place to try new skills, perhaps fail at first, practise and try again, as well as to succeed).

In my experience, the following qualities are also important in potential team members. They should:

- Have a desire to be part of a team

- Be reliable and dependable

- Exhibit a degree of enthusiasm

- Be appropriate to the sex of the children attending. It is wise as far as possible to have female leaders if you are running a girls only club. Mixed clubs and boys only clubs can have a mixture of male and female leaders – try and avoid all female leaders in this context if possible because it is good for boys to have a positive male role-model.

This list looks rather awesome, and you might wonder whether you'll ever find enough people to make up your team with these attributes. You do need to be realistic. Of course you cannot wait until you have found the ideal team full of gifted children's workers before you start up a club – you'd probably never get it going! Beware of trying to look for people who exhibit all of these qualities now. Some of the qualifications can be viewed as what you would eventually be aiming at for the team, rather than qualities which are there at the start. And some people may well have these qualities already, but they might not be immediately obvious on first meeting – they may seem unlikely children's workers, and yet prove to be brilliant. This again confirms the importance of appropriate training for the team, to which we will now turn.

Training

Training can be formal or informal, and probably in practice should be a combination of the two. It should also ideally take place over a period of time so that individuals have the opportunity to learn and then put what they've learnt into practice before learning more. Training is something which we can never say that we've done and need no more of. Whatever stage we are at, it is to the detriment of our work if at any time we feel we have 'made it' and learnt all that there is to learn.

Examples of formal training are an individual reading relevant books, attending training sessions put on either within or outside the Church, asking for advice or instruction from a more experienced and knowledgeable children's worker, a correspondence course, or even taking time out to attend an appropriate residential course to give a formal qualification. In terms of your leadership team, I have found it is a good idea to put on a formal training session of some type once a quarter. In practice it is unlikely that the whole team will be able to make every session and so this means that hopefully all team members are having at least a couple of formal training sessions a year. This could be an evening session or a half-day, and might involve having a speaker either from outside or within the church talking on a particular aspect of the work. See the entry for chapter 4 in the bibliography at the back of this book for lists of various agencies who provide training services, and of training packs, programmes and manuals which are available for you to use as individuals or as a team.

Informal training takes place alongside, and often in the course of, running the club and doing the work itself. Individually, it is good for team members to be encouraged to reflect upon the part they have played in the club, and how they would change or improve it for next time. There are also many opportunities to learn as you work together as a team with the children. A few minutes together before the club session starts to discuss the evening's programme and everyone's role is very useful. It is also a good idea to have a debriefing and evaluating time after each club, and a longer session at the end of each term. This is an opportunity to provide helpful feedback for members of the team as to how parts of the session went. Talk about things which worked well, what did not work so well and any improvements or refinements for next time. Some good informal training can be done in this way.

At the outset you will probably want to get the team together for a number of sessions, many of which will be informal discussion-type meetings sorting out basic principles and issues (you could, for instance, get together to discuss the questions on pages 7 and 9–11), and some of which will be formal training sessions. With a new team, you might want to spend time doing some team-building exercises, and getting to know each other. It is important that the team is as well-prepared as possible before you actually start running the club for the first time – there will be less time once the club has got underway.

"debriefing and evaluation time"

The first decisions

Once you have got your leadership team together, basic decisions such as the age-group you are going to concentrate on initially, the day and time of your club, as well as approaching the appropriate sources for financial help, need to be made together. It might be that you will need to have had at least a vague idea of your initial target age-group before getting the leadership team together, so that appropriately gifted leaders can be found. It is rather a chicken and egg situation.

Decisions such as age-group, day and time should be made primarily by answering questions like those at the end of chapter 1 (page 7). Hopefully answering these will help you to find out the age range, and the most appropriate day and time for the children of this age, in your target area. The leadership must also be taken into consideration – not only their areas of expertise as regards age-group, but also the day and time most suitable for them to commit themselves on a regular basis. Another relevant consideration is the availability of a suitable venue. If your church does not have a suitable building, it is often feasible to ask to have it in a local school hall, village hall, youth club, scout hut, etc. Fundamental considerations for the suitability of a venue are the availability of toilets and running water and the safety of the premises (although most venues can be made safe); most other considerations are secondary. Your church calendar such as church meetings, PCCs and prayer meetings must also be taken into account when considering the proposed day and timing of the club sessions.

If your church has a mission statement, see how the children's work upon which you are about to embark fits into it. If there is no mention of children's work specifically, perhaps you could encourage the church to include its work with children in the statement. The club leadership team might also want to draw up their own mission statement and see where and how the rest of the church fits in.

Publicity, parental consent and prayer

Once decisions like age, day, time and place have been made, you need to go public, and as public as possible! The more people who know about what you are planning to do the better. You could have small invitations with the appropriate details on them made to hand to children or parents, as well as posters and handbills. You could make your own, or the Christian Publicity Organisation sells a variety of good publicity material (address in the entry for this chapter in the bibliography). Schools may allow you to go and publicise in person, or agree to pass on invitations to every child

in the school. You could also pass on invitations through the other contacts you have – church activities, uniformed organisations, etc. A local paper feature may also be a good idea. This publicity launch needs to be done about a month in advance, depending upon the time of year. You need to strike a balance between giving people enough time to register the event and then decide to come, and giving too much time so that although at the time the idea seemed a good one it is all too far away to make any decisions yet, and once the time arrives, the publicity has been forgotten.

At some stage, parental consent is required for each child attending. You may like to know definite numbers before you start. If this is the case, you need to mention on your publicity how parents are to go about registering their children by signing a consent form before the first club. If you do not need to know in advance how many children might come, the consent forms could be given to parents to fill in as they bring their children for the first session – if so, then you'll need to say something to the effect of 'just turn up!' on the publicity.

Although there will have been much prayer already surrounding the project, now is also a good time to get people to support the club regularly in prayer as it actually takes place week by week. Prayer is a vital key to the success of the club – it is God's work, and we must be constantly turning to Him to ask Him to work in the lives of these children through us, and to equip and enable us.

CHAPTER 5
Planning a Programme

The content of the programme you put on for the children week by week is vital in two major respects. First, it is the activities that you do and the level of enjoyment for the children that will determine the success of the club as far as they are concerned. It is the key to whether or not they will really look forward to coming each week. Second, if our aim is to teach children about the Christian faith, then our programmes must not only be appropriate and fun, but must supremely be encouraging the children to learn about the Christian faith. The programme as a whole must be an effective way of communicating what we want the children to discover week by week.

"drama and role play"

How children learn

Learning by discovery or active learning is the most effective way a child both learns and remembers. Active learning means that children learn by doing. Children take in:

10% of what they hear

50% of what they see

60% of what they say

90% of what they do.

Children learn by listening to stories told with enthusiasm. Telling stories will probably be the main way of 'directive' teaching we employ during a session. Young children learn by hearing things over and over again – repetition. Learning by ear alone is, however, limited. Children of all ages learn more from looking and hearing than hearing alone. Using visual aids

when telling stories enhances understanding, aids concentration and increases interest. When children have the opportunity to say what they have understood it enables the leader to know if learning has taken place – you can use quizzes, drama, memory work, discussion, or question and answer to do this. However, more is remembered and understood from doing than from any other form of learning. This can be achieved by having a varied programme of games, drama, role-play, craft, quizzes, etc., all with the aim of communicating the truth being studied from the Bible material. Incorporating a range of all these different activities (hearing, looking, saying and doing) into a programme will aid learning and provide an enjoyable club for the children.

The club session itself is relatively short, so ideally the children need to be given just one main idea or teaching point to take away with them. Some children might well remember every detail of the story we present or the games we play. But on the whole, most will learn and remember much more effectively if one truth is taught through a variety of different activities. A good teaching programme is one which will incorporate many different types of activities, all communicating one teaching point.

A balanced programme

It is important that the programme is well-balanced in all respects. As far as teaching themes are concerned, the programme should be balanced in terms of content over a period of say a year. The programme also needs to be balanced in terms of the different types of activities in one evening (this is easier to manage with some teaching themes than others). Ideally, you would have a range of quiet and more active, individual and team activities in one evening. It also widens the variety for children if you include some areas of choice on occasions. It is a good idea to make room for individual children's needs and interests if possible. If you have enough leaders, you do not need to insist that all of the children take part in all of the activities – it's good to spare an extra leader to be alongside the odd child not participating on occasions. It adds to the level of interest and enjoyment for the children if you include some off-site activities during the term as well, such as swimming, sports hall visits and trips to parks. Although this can bring practical difficulties of transport and cost, in my experience it is well worth while for the extra pleasure the children get out of it. It enhances greatly the group dynamics and also gives opportunities for building good relationships – the leaders with the children and the children with each other.

How will the children respond?

It will not always be easy to know how the children will respond to your programme. How do you know whether they have enjoyed the club session you have painstakingly prepared? Some children will be more outwardly enthusiastic than

"more outwardly enthusiastic than others"

others. We cannot expect all the children to enjoy everything all of the time, and some children might be enjoying themselves despite trying to give you the opposite impression (this is boring, do we have to do this? . . . etc.). If the children come back week after week, that is a pretty sure sign that what you are doing is good.

What if some of the children misbehave?

Human nature means that at times children will be destructive, silly, selfish and disrespectful. Therefore you will need to have a discipline strategy so that behaviour is changed for the better, and so that your work is not hindered and other children put off coming.

Children derive security from knowing where the boundaries are and who is able to enforce them. So decide on your basic rules before you start – what behaviour will not be acceptable, and what you will do with children who disobey. Make these rules clear to the children so that they know what is expected of them. Children thrive best in an atmosphere of genuine love, undergirded by reasonable, consistent discipline. It is therefore good to have discussed a policy for discipline with all of the leaders beforehand, so that there is consistency amongst you – otherwise children can play one leader off against another. It is the ultimate paradox of childhood that although youngsters want to be led, they insist that the people who lead them earn that right. So expect more confrontations in the early stages of your work – the children will probably want to test out the firmness of your boundaries. Many confrontations can be avoided by building friendships with the children and thereby making them want to co-operate with you. Children learn what they are taught – in the area of behaviour too. Leaders should be a good example to the children in every way, including respecting them and disciplining wisely. There should be mutual respect between children and leaders. Developing respect for leaders is critical – if leaders are not respected, neither will their values and beliefs.

Reasons for discipline problems

There can be various reasons for discipline failing. Some of the main ones are:

◆ Poor programme: can result in boredom and disruption.

◆ Leader's approach: too authoritarian can result in aggression, too laid back can result in misbehaviour – either way enjoyment for children is spoiled.

- Differences in children: individuals react and behave differently, and so they cannot be treated in the same way.

- Inconsistency: no clear boundaries or irregular discipline result in confusion and children will behave as they wish.

Solutions to discipline problems

- Create an interesting programme
- Create clear boundaries
- Know your children
- Plan a discipline strategy
- Evaluate
- Pray

Restrictions and limitations to your programme

There will be certain limitations to be taken into account when it comes to planning the specific details of the programme. The main ones (not necessarily in order of magnitude of restriction) are:

- Finances: the money available to you to spend on each club session might affect the materials you can use in craft activities, games you can play, etc.

- Venue: the place where you meet might be a limitation in terms of the activities that it is unfeasible or unsafe to attempt, e.g. cooking, active games, indoor and outdoor games. Some activities can be adapted, or perhaps on the odd occasion for something special, an alternative venue could be used.

- Resources: it will probably take time to build up a supply of good and useful resources, unless your church or organisation is fortunate enough to have some already. Make the most of people's cast-offs – old footballs, tennis balls, empty yoghurt pots, toilet roll middles, etc. Sometimes schools or offices get rid of old scissors, paper cutters, photocopiers, paper or furniture. Make it known that you are on the look-out for these things and involve as many people as you can in helping to find them.

- Time: the amount of time leaders can offer will have an influence upon the type of programme you can offer. Good programmes do take a lot of preparation time (and some clearing away time). You can share out the different activities for preparation amongst the leaders. It is also possible to give things to other people to do who will not be there on the day, but would have the time and ability to do something in advance – I have often found this very useful in terms of visual aids, pictures, a demonstration craft activity, etc.

- Children: the children, what they do and do not enjoy, and their particular limitations (e.g. being poor readers) will affect the type of programme you will be able to put on. It may well take time to find out exactly what works well with a particular group of children and what does not. In the early stages be on the look-out for things which have worked well and not so well – it is a good idea to keep some type of list for future reference. Occasionally activities do not work well on a particular night for one reason or another, but might do if tried again on a different evening. Sometimes you will not know if something doesn't work until the activity itself has been a bit of a disaster, and you will know for next time. Although it is disappointing to have spent time and energy preparing a game or activity which hasn't worked well, this is to be expected now and again – working with people will always to some extent be unpredictable, and is not always due to poor preparation or presentation (although sometimes it can be – see the following section on organisation and management).

- The material: whatever material you use, expect to have to adapt it. This is because no material can possibly take into account all the limitations described above, and all the different circumstances that individual clubs will come across. Some material will need minor alterations, and some more major changes. Do not be afraid to adapt the ideas if you think other things might work better with your group.

Organisation and management

A good club programme needs very good organisation. The amount of time you invest in preparing everything down to the last detail will reap great benefits during the session itself. If you're spending time while the children are there getting things ready, the evening will soon lose its flow, the children may get bored and that will lead to either disillusionment and/or discipline problems. The leaders should all know beforehand their specific responsibilities for the evening, and make sure that they have everything prepared for what they are doing. As far as management is concerned, the evening usually works better if there is one leader in overall responsibility (it need not necessarily be the same leader each week) and in charge of co-ordinating the time between all the activities, the changeovers and timing for the evening.

Evaluation and assessment

It is a good idea to assess and evaluate the session after it is over. If all the leaders can do this together at some stage then it should provide a broad, balanced view of the evening – everyone will have a slightly different perspective on what has happened and how the evening went. Note any changes, games that were successful, craft ideas that worked well, particular discipline problems, etc. for the future (and make a note of the activities you should not try again too!).

CHAPTER 6
Parts of the Programme

As mentioned earlier, everything in the club programme should focus on the truth from the Bible that you want to impart to the children (the teaching point of the session). Therefore, as long as all your activities have this purpose in mind, you can do almost anything – the more creative, entertaining and relevant for the children the better! In your club session, you might want to include a tea break – time to relax with a cup of squash and a biscuit, or even have a tuck shop where the children can buy biscuits, cans or chocolate. You might also want to have a 'social' or off-site session once in a while (say every three weeks). This could be swimming, a trip to the cinema or a sports hall. As far as the teaching goes, there are certain standard activities which you will probably want to include on a fairly regular basis in order to fulfil the objectives outlined above. They are stories (or presentation of the Bible material), games, craft/art and music/singing. Depending upon your group you might also want to include prayer, puzzle sheets and memory work too. There are a few comments on each of these different parts of the programme in the following section.

Telling stories

The story or Bible material presentation is the heart of the club session. Out of the whole club programme it is the main way that the Bible material is imparted and the teaching point of the session given. As it is a vital part of the club, the children should be gripped by it, and therefore it needs a lot of planning, preparation and creativity.

Children (and adults) love stories. You have a marvellous opportunity every session to tell the children part of the best story of all – the true story of God's plan for humanity from creation, fall, through rescue to life with Him for ever. How can you make sure the children get the most out of this vital part of the club programme? Here are some basic principles to bear in mind when telling a story:

◆ Eye contact is very important – this ideally means that stories should be told without a script or book. It comes to life much more if it is told directly, and you can also build up a much better rapport with the children, as well as being able to observe their reactions. You should also be on their level when telling a story, i.e. sitting down with them, not standing over them.

◆ It is important that the children know that this is a story from the Bible – not just one that you have made up. You could have the Bible open on your lap, or make some reference to specific verses, without reading directly from it all the time.

◆ Be enthusiastic yourself about it – enthusiasm is infectious.

- Make sure that the story interests and excites you – if it doesn't it probably will not interest and excite them either.

- Be confident. With most stories the really important part is the main point, so don't worry if when you first start you get some of the details wrong or miss things out.

- Include the children as much as possible without ruining the flow, with responses, actions, questions.

- Think of how the story relates to the child's experience, and apply the story in a relevant way to their experience.

- Be as visual as possible. We live in a visual age, and children have come to rely greatly upon visual images.

THE TOWER OF GAGEL...

'What's the use of a book, thought Alice, without pictures or conversations?' So writes Lewis Carroll at the beginning of *Alice in Wonderland*. As well as hearing good stories, children also love seeing or doing whilst listening. Using at least one of the other four senses (as well as hearing) during the Bible material presentation will mean that the child will enjoy, concentrate and remember the story better. There are a few people who in telling a story can captivate their audience simply with facial expressions and voice intonation. But on the whole, the story will be more enjoyable for the children and will achieve more if you use other resources to help you in your story telling.

The basic rule is to be as creative and imaginative as you can in the way you present the Bible material, without detracting from the story itself. Choose appropriate ideas that will reinforce the message of the story – you want the children to remember the story as a whole, not just the activity running alongside it. Here are some ideas that are tried and tested just for starters – think of new and different ideas yourself!

Puppets

Glove, finger, box, wooden spoon, sock – there are many different sorts to make yourself or buy. Perhaps the children could make them as part of their craft, and use them in the story? It's important to practise using puppets on your own (in front of a mirror?) before using them in front of the children.

Masks

Similar to puppets – the easiest sort can be made from paper plates. You can wear them or get the children to wear them. Masks can be made yourself or by the children. An alternative to masks are paper plates with faces for different moods – angry, sad, happy, etc. These can be used for bringing out the emotions of the character(s) in the story.

In character

Dress up as a character in the story, and tell the story from their point of view.

Hats

A different hat for a different character. This needs practice beforehand, and a good supply of varied hats, bought or made, is needed.

Models

Models can be used very successfully, although they are often rather time-consuming to prepare. Ideas are lego or duplo model houses 'built' on a mound of sand or on a large flat stone and pouring water from a jug at the appropriate moment – the story of the two builders (Luke 6.48-49); a large boat made from card and/or cardboard boxes (big enough for children to sit in) with canes and string for fishing rod – stories of Jesus and the disciples fishing.

Responses

Some stories lend themselves to this idea more than others. If there are a few words which appear several times in the story, teach the children a response to do each time that word appears, such as waves – whoosh!, etc.

Prop boxes

Look through the story and choose appropriate items to pull out of a large box as you tell the story, for example bread, a tin of sardines, a napkin, a thermos and a lunch box could all feature in a story about the feeding of the five thousand.

Pictures

These need to be fairly large so that every child can see them, and require a fair measure of artistic skill, although there are ways to cheat – tracing, using an OHP to enlarge, or enlarging existing illustrations on a photocopier. Clip-art books are especially useful as they usually allow you to photocopy and use the material without breaching any copyright. Look through children's books to give you creative ideas: opening up flaps to reveal something underneath, finding something that is hidden in the picture, etc.

Story friezes

A large roll of paper can be used to illustrate scenes from the story. It is unrolled gradually to reveal the next picture or part of the story.

Story cubes

Six pictures are glued onto the sides of a large box or cube. Turn the box to the appropriate picture as you tell the story.

Story lines

Have a clothes-line, and paint pictures and the occasional word on pieces of paper for the children to peg up at the appropriate place in the story.

Overhead projector

This can be used in several ways: colour pictures copied or traced from books, adding or removing overlays during the story with one existing piece remaining throughout (this works very well with the creation story for example) and simple silhouette figures or pieces can be used, with a colour background if appropriate. Changing the pictures needs to be practised in advance.

Drama, mime or role-play

Both leaders and/or children can be used to act out stories. Children can be given words in advance (if appropriate) or asked to improvise. You could video it if a video camera is available so that the children can watch themselves later – a good means of reinforcing the story.

Interviews

A leader can interview a character in the story (who can be another leader or a child) and can describe what has happened, how they feel, and so on.

Surprise messages

Get a leader to knock on the door and present, for example, a razor or pair of scissors with a note attached saying, 'Dear children, as I slept last night some men came and used these on my hair – can you find out who I am and what will happen to me now? Try looking on page . . . in your Bible.' Get the children (or a leader) to look up the story and continue it.

Flash cards

This idea is only appropriate for children who can read. Simple phrases or words which are repeated in the story can be written clearly on card and held up at the appropriate time in the story, to reinforce that phrase or word. The children could be asked to shout out the phrase or word all together.

Choral poems or raps

Again, only appropriate for good readers, and certain stories. The story is written (in large script) on a big piece of paper in verse, usually involving some sort of repetitive chorus. The children are invited to say the poem all together. It could be taped so that the children can listen as it is played back which again is a good means of reinforcing the story.

Sound

Stories which involve lots of different sounds can be told very effectively using the children to make the appropriate sounds whilst the story is being told. Or you could give a copy of the story to the children and get them to make a soundtrack for it in groups on their own. It can be performed, taped and played back as many times as you want!

Story games

Some games lend themselves to incorporating a story – pass the parcel with a part of the story in each layer; hunting for different parts of the story around the room and putting it together in the right order; putting selected pictures or words from the story out on the table and the children have to stick them on a piece of paper at the other end of the room when that part of the story is mentioned – the list is endless! On the whole the more lively the game, the more appropriate it is for reinforcement of the story rather than the only way the story is presented. If you want to play a lively game, first get the children to listen to the story once (at least) to start with, so that it is familiar and the message is not lost in the general excitement and enthusiasm of the game.

Preparing a story

1. Read the Bible passage through a few times to familiarise yourself with it.

What is the main point of the passage or the point that you are going to concentrate on from the passage? (There may be many things – choose only one.)

How does the story relate to the child's experience? How can you make it relevant to the child by relating it to his/her experience?

2. Look carefully at the passage and find any words which the children might not understand. Either replace these words with more familiar ones with the same meaning, or remember to explain the meaning of the words when you come to them in the story. Words you might feel that it is important to explain are ones which will be useful to them in the future if they can understand now what they mean, such as sin.

3. Decide upon an idea of visual presentation for the story.

4. Read the passage over so that you know the story well, the main facts, the order of events. Decide what is important to the story, and what

is not so vital taking into account the message you want to communicate. Remember that it is better to have a story that is slightly too short than so long that children lose concentration and miss the message.

5. Prepare the story for telling so that it has:

◆ An interesting, action-packed beginning

◆ A rapid progression of events with vivid description

◆ A climax or high point

◆ A short, clear ending

◆ The main point or message stated clearly as many times as is appropriate during the story

◆ The main point applied appropriately with reference to the children's experience

◆ Some questions for discussion at the end.

Write it down if it will help you to remember it.

6. Read it through as many times as is necessary for you to be able to tell the story without looking at the paper. Practise without the paper, and then with the visual aids. If you are not confident of remembering everything, make a list of cue words.

7. Use your voice in telling the story – tone, pitch and pace are important.

8. Pray.

9. Enjoy the story and learn from it yourself as you are telling it to the children.

"contact games best avoided"

Games

Playing games as part of the club programme can be much more than just enjoyable time-fillers for the children. The main teaching point we are trying to communicate in your club session can be brought alive by playing appropriate games.

Games can become learning experiences where the children discover things for themselves in a real and tangible way. They also have the advantage of not relying heavily upon a high degree of literacy, unlike other aids to learning we might include in the programme.

Games are extremely versatile – they can liven up an evening or calm things down. Competitive games can build team spirit, develop skill and sharpen mind and body, but they can lead to name-calling and feelings of inferiority. You therefore need to be aware of individuals' characteristics and needs and be sensitive to them. Most team or competitive games can be adapted if you wish to play non-competitively. You also need to be aware of potential problems caused by playing 'contact' games, and these may be best avoided, at least until the group is established.

The real importance of the games as far as the programme is concerned is in the application, and the discussion and thinking time afterwards. It is only when the games are applied effectively that they become part of an active learning process. So if you are planning a game, spend time thinking about the application, and how you will draw out in discussion or some other way the relevance of the game for the children as far as the teaching programme is concerned.

Craft activities

Most children enjoy making things – especially items that they can use or eat! I haven't yet come across a child who doesn't enjoy cooking, and although you might have limited facilities on-site, it is possible to do some type of cooking whatever your venue is like. With some groups of children, or for certain craft activities, you might want to provide a choice of other activities for those who would prefer not to make something. It is also good to have another activity ready for children who finish the craft activity very quickly. Some will quite happily spend as much time as they're allowed to putting the final touches to their work of art, and others will try to finish as quickly as possible.

Singing and music

Most young children (under seven) enjoy singing and making music. It might not appeal to some groups, such as older boys, but most groups enjoy making music or using instruments to make sound effects for a story. Singing songs based around the teaching theme is a very good way of helping children to remember the material, and take it away with them. You can also tape it and play it back as many times as they want to.

Memory work

Asking the children to learn certain Bible verses and remember them for the next week can be a good way of helping them remember the material, but again this might be more appropriate with some groups than with others. You can make the learning (and remembering the following week) of the verses fun, so that the children enjoy it. As long as it is not something that you do every week, memory verses work really well with some groups – it is especially good for those children who cannot read because it helps them to learn Bible truths that they cannot read for themselves. The remembering of the verses should be optional.

Prayer

Running clubs often means that you are working with children who do not know what being a follower of Jesus means or have made no decision to follow him themselves. Even at a fairly young age, some children will already have decided that they do not believe in Jesus, they do not wish to follow him or they are not quite sure. This is especially the case for children who come from homes where their parents are not believers. You might think that it is inappropriate to put these children in a position where they feel obliged to participate in something that they do not believe in, such as prayer. One way of overcoming this is by prefacing your prayer with a sentence like this: 'I'm going to say a short prayer/talk to God now. If you want to pray too, listen to what I say, and if you agree with it say Amen. If you don't want to pray or talk to God, just keep very still and quiet so you don't disturb those who do.' Alternatively, you might think it appropriate not to pray as a large group together, but to give an opportunity at some stage for children to pray with a leader if they would like to.

Puzzles and fun sheets

Some children really enjoy doing wordsearches, puzzles and colouring in pictures on worksheets centred around the teaching theme for the session. There are whole books of these available (for example, the *Instant Art for Bible Worksheets* series, published by Palm Tree Press) which are free of copyright for photocopying. For some children these are too much like school work and can really put them off – so get to know your group before using them, and if they are a problem use them only occasionally, have them as an optional activity or use them as 'take home' sheets.

Quizzes

Having some type of quiz is a very good way of reinforcing what the children have discovered in the session. Use as many different ways as possible of presenting the quiz and a variety of methods of scoring to make them lots of fun for the children. You could sometimes have a quiz at the end of the story, or at the end of the whole session. When doing a series which requires continuity between sessions, such as the life of David, I have often found it helpful to start a session with a quiz recapping the material from the previous week's session. This also provides an opportunity for those who were not present at the previous week's session to catch up on what they have missed, and provides a good way-in to this week's session for all the children.

PART 2

The Programme Pages

Using the Programme Pages

For the sake of simplicity (and to save my type-weary fingers!), I have referred to all the children in the programme pages as 'he'. This term is, of course, intended to include both boys and girls.

All Bible passages and verses quoted are from the International Children's Bible (ICB) (New Century Version, Anglicised Edition, 1991, Nelson Word Ltd). This is an excellent translation as it is the only one written solely for children from the original Hebrew and Greek texts, and as such it is highly recommended for use in all work with children and young people.

As with all teaching material, you should expect to have to adapt parts of the programme pages which follow to suit your own group of children, the venue, the leaders, finances available, etc.

There is enough material in these pages for three terms of weekly clubs, with nine teaching sessions in each term. If you are intending to run your club to fit in with school terms, the material will be sufficient as long as you have some social events in your term programme. You might also want to have some kind of celebration at the end of each term – a party on the last session before Christmas, an Easter Egg Hunt, and a barbecue or beach party at the end of the other two terms, for example. With older groups (7-10s) weekend 'sleepovers' at your club venue or away somewhere can provide excellent opportunities both for furthering relationships and providing good teaching experiences.

Each session in the programme pages includes in detail ideas for the basic parts of the programme discussed earlier in the book – games, story and craft activities. There are also extra suggestions for appropriate songs and bible verses to fit in with the theme of the session. Most of the games and activities have been devised with non-readers and non-writers in mind. This has been my intention for two reasons. First, in this way it is suitable for younger as well as older children. Second, it also appeals to older children who do not enjoy or are not able to use these skills. In my own club work with different groups of children in the past, I have always found it easier to find or think of reading/writing activities to supplement an existing programme than to find or

think of activities which do not require reading and writing skills. There are many books available which contain various types of photocopiable puzzle sheets or worksheets to add to existing programmes. See the entry in the bibliography for chapter 6 for a full list.

Each printed session lasts an hour, although the times given for the various activities are approximate. Most club sessions usually last from between an hour to an hour and a half. Extra time is needed at the start of the session for registration and so on, and you might also decide to have a refreshment break or tuck shop. So in practice, you might well not have time for everything that you want to include and occasionally you might need to leave some items out.

The activities in each session are written in the order in which they are to be done. They are divided into the following categories:

Way-In

These are designed as warm-up exercises to enable the children to start thinking around the theme or to introduce the theme of the session. If you are short of time, you may want to have fewer of these activities than is sometimes suggested in the material. It is however vital to have at least one activity like this, as the children benefit greatly from it both in terms of warm-up and preparation for the story.

Story

This is the main way in which the Bible material is presented to the children, and should have as much visual input as possible. Some of the ideas given earlier in the book might be of use. It is also important that the teaching is applied to the children appropriately, so that it is relevant to their experience. With most groups of children, some type of discussion after the story will enable you to determine how much the children have understood. Recalling the information will also help the children remember it more readily.

The length and level of discussion will vary greatly from group to group and even sometimes from session to session. Adapt the questions and the period after the story to suit your group, and to some extent be prepared to play it by ear!

Follow-up

These are activities which are designed to reinforce the teaching theme and help to apply the teaching for the children. As these are on the whole craft activities, you might want to omit them with some groups of children who do not particularly enjoy them. You can supplement the programme with the full range of Way-In activities, or perhaps some kind of puzzle or fun sheet, a quiz, singing or memory verse.

Songs

There are a few suggestions for appropriate songs at the end of most of the sessions. They are drawn from Junior Praise (JP), Mission Praise (MP), Songs of Fellowship for Kids (SFK), and Kids Praise (KP).

Bible verses

There are some suggestions from the ICB of appropriate bible verses that could be used as memory verses for the children to learn.

Symbols

In the programme pages:

 denotes some type of game, and

 is a type of craft activity.

Many of the team games or competitive games can be adapted fairly easily if you would rather the children play non-competitively (see section on games page 29). Some games and craft activities are given alternatives for different age groups. These age groupings are only approximate, so choose the option which is most likely to suit your group of children. With craft activities, you might like to give the children the choice of either activity.

I hope that you and the children in your club enjoy using these programme pages!

David, the man who loved God

How God chose a new King

1 Samuel 16.1-13

Bible Theme
*People look on the outside,
God looks at the heart*

Way-In
Grab it!

(5 mins)

You will need: *A tray of several small 'goodies' – one item for each child (one could be a chocolate bar, several wrapped sweets, etc.)*

Make sure that one item is a piece of plasticene with a £1 or 50p coin hidden inside it.

The tray is covered up whilst you explain to the children that when you uncover the tray, they will have 10 seconds to grab whatever they would like. They are only allowed to grab one item. Whatever they grab, they can keep.

After the game, talk about how they made their choices and why they decided to grab that item. Then show what is inside the plasticene. What did it look like on the outside? Which was the most valuable item?

Way-In
Pass the parcels

(15 mins)

You will need:
Newspaper
Bar of chocolate
Dirty old cloth
Attractive wrapping-up paper

Wrap up two parcels; one wrapped in newspaper containing the chocolate bar, the other wrapped up in attractive paper containing the old cloth. Play pass the parcel with both parcels at the same time.

When you have finished, talk about the difference between what the parcels looked like on the outside and what they were like on the inside.

Story and discussion

(10 mins)

Tell the story with as much visual input as possible. One idea might be to let the children act this story out. I have sometimes varied the detail slightly by making each brother an expert at something, such as being very strong, very clever, very sporty, or very handsome. Provide suitable costumes if possible. David is very young, and not especially good at anything, but he does love God, which was why God chose him.

Discuss or ask these questions afterwards. Make the link with the two games.

1. How did God decide who to choose as his new King?

2. What does God think is more important – what we look like or what we are like as a person?

Follow-up Run and choose

(10 mins)

You will need:
Magazines and newspapers
Scissors
Glue
Card

Cut out pictures of various types of people from the magazines and newspapers. Make sure some look 'good' and some look 'not so good'.

Stick each picture on a small piece of card. You need one picture for each child who plays the game.

Divide the children into two teams. Put enough people on cards for each child in the team and place these at the opposite end of the room to the team.

Play this as a team game, getting each child to run up and collect a card and bring it back to the team.

4-6s When they have collected all the cards, the team must put them in a long line and sit around them in a circle. The first team to do this is the winning team.

Then talk about how the people on the cards look different on the outside, but only God knows what they're really like as people (on the inside), which is the most important.

7-10s When they have collected all the cards, the team must place them in the order in which they would choose the person to be king.

Talk about how they decided upon an order. Although the people looked different on the outside, only God knows what they are really like on the inside – and this is more important.

Follow-Up Sheep and gates mobile

(20 mins)

You will need:
Templates (see opposite)
Coloured and white card
Cotton wool
Glue
Cotton
Pencils
Scissors

The children make a mobile by tracing around the templates and cutting out the sheep and gates. They should stick the cotton wool on the sheep templates, and use the coloured card for the gates. A leader or the child should attach the cotton to the sheep and gates to make a mobile.

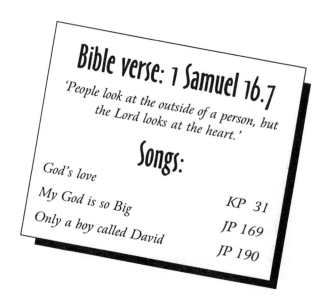

Bible verse: 1 Samuel 16.7
'People look at the outside of a person, but the Lord looks at the heart.'

Songs:

God's love
My God is so Big   KP 31
Only a boy called David   JP 169
                           JP 190

SESSION 2

David and Goliath

1 Samuel 17

Bible Theme
*God is powerful,
He defeated Goliath*

Way-In
Can you hit the target?

(10 mins)

You will need:
*A large (A2) piece of paper
Tubes of smarties*

Draw a 'target' on the sheet of paper. You will need one target per group of six children.

Put the target on the floor and get the children to sit about 2m away from it, in a line.

Give each child five smarties of the same colour (a different colour for each child).

The children take it in turns to roll one of their smarties onto the target and see what they can score. The leader can keep a record of the scores.

The winner is the child with the highest score from rolling all five smarties.

Story and discussion

(10 mins)

Tell the story with as much visual input as possible. (One idea is to use a prop box with sandwiches, armour, a sling, small pebbles, etc. inside.)

Questions for discussion:

1. How did David beat Goliath?

2. How did God help David to beat Goliath?

3. Discuss the ways God can help us when we are in trouble.

Follow-up
Knock him over!

(10 mins)

You will need:
*Bean bags or soft balls
Cardboard boxes
Plank of wood, or bamboo canes*

Make a very large (3m tall!) Goliath from a strip of cardboard. Use a plank of wood, or bamboo canes stuck in the middle of Goliath's back to give the model support.

The children take it in turns to stand a distance away, and try to knock Goliath over using a bean bag or a soft ball. (The easiest way to do this obviously is to aim for his head to try to topple him over!)

Follow-up Build him up and knock him down

(10 mins)

You will need: Enough boxes for each team to pile one on top of the other. Draw an outline of Goliath on each tower of boxes.

This is a team game. Unstack the boxes and put them at the opposite end of the room to the teams.

The children have to run and fetch a box one at a time, bring it back to their team and then stack it in the right order to make Goliath.

When they have done this, the smallest child from the team runs to the other end of the room and tries to knock Goliath over by throwing a bean bag or sponge ball at the boxes.

The first team to knock Goliath down is the winning team.

Follow-Up Painting pebbles

(20 mins)

God used David's pebble to beat Goliath. What can you use a pebble to make?

You will need:
Pebbles/stones
Enamel paint
Brushes
Varnish

The children paint their own designs on the stones, using enamel paint (see suggestions below).

After they have dried, they can be varnished.

41

Saul tries to kill David

1 Samuel 18,19

Bible Theme
God looks after those who trust Him

Way-In
Dodge ball

(5 mins)

You will need:
A large foam/soft ball

This game can be played indoors or outdoors. The children stand in a group in the middle of the room. The leaders stand in a ring around the outside of the children. (If you have less than 4 leaders you can split the group of children into two teams and have one team in the middle and the other team in a ring around the outside. Play the game once and then swap over.)

The leader with the ball must roll it across the circle to another leader.

The children must 'dodge' or jump over the ball so that it does not touch them below the knee. If it does touch a child below the knee then that child is out of the game and either joins the leaders around the group, or sits out.

The leaders continue rolling the ball until only one child is left.

Story and discussion

(10 mins)

Talk about the game the children have just played. David spent many years dodging and trying to get away. In his case it was not dodging from a ball, but from Saul, who was trying to kill him.

Tell the story with as much visual input as possible. (One idea is to have a surprise message sent from David to the children, saying that someone is trying to kill him.)

Questions for discussion:

1. Who did David depend on to keep him safe?

2. How did God keep David safe?

3. Discuss the kinds of situations in which the children need to be kept safe. Who can they trust to look after them?

Follow-Up
Running wordsearch
(7-10s) **or**
Picture race
(4-6s)

(15 mins)

7-10s

You will need:
A Wordsearch
Large sheets of paper
Large marker pen

Write out the Wordsearch on a large piece of paper (A2). You might need more than one if you have over eight children.

Draw a picture of each of the words in the Wordsearch on separate pieces of paper. These pictures should be at the opposite end of the room to the children.

4-6s

Draw pictures of some of the words from the story on these sheets of paper.

Put the pictures at the opposite end of the room to where the children are sitting.

Both

The children gather together (7-10s around the Wordsearch) as a leader reads or tells the story again.

7-10s When the leader comes to a word which is in the Wordsearch, he pauses to enable the children to search for the word. When someone finds it, they circle it, and then run to collect the picture from the other end of the room.

4-6s When the leader comes to a word which has a picture, he pauses so that a child can run to the other end of the room and find the right picture. The children take it in turns to run for the picture.

Both The leader waits until they have found the word and collected the right picture before carrying on with the story.

S	A	M	U	E	L	Y	I	J
A	T	S	I	L	T	O	N	O
U	I	D	O	L	R	E	S	N
L	I	A	N	H	A	R	P	A
F	E	V	E	T	R	I	E	T
S	K	I	L	L	S	T	A	H
B	E	D	I	L	L	S	R	A
E	S	C	A	P	E	D	X	N
F	W	I	N	D	O	W	Y	E

Hidden words: kill, David, Saul, Jonathan, harp, spear, window, escaped, idol, bed, Samuel

Follow-up
Burst it!

(10 mins)

You will need:
A balloon per child
About 50cm of string per child

Older children can blow up their own balloon. The other end of the string is tied to the child's ankle.

The children must try and burst each other's balloons by treading on them, whilst protecting their own balloon from being burst.

When a child's balloon is burst, he is out of the game, and cannot continue trying to burst others' balloons.

The winner is the child with his balloon left at the end.

Follow-Up
A safekeeping box

(20 mins)

You will need:
Card
Box template (see overleaf)
Paint – spray, powder, enamel or poster
Paint brushes
Scissors
Glue

The template should be photocopied onto card for the children before the session.

The children cut out the template (for younger children you might need to do this for them before the session) and fold it as shown.

The children stick the box together and then paint it.

Bible verse: Proverbs 29.25
'Whoever trusts in the Lord is kept safe.'

Songs:
Come on, let's go for it KP 9
When the road is rough and steep JP 279

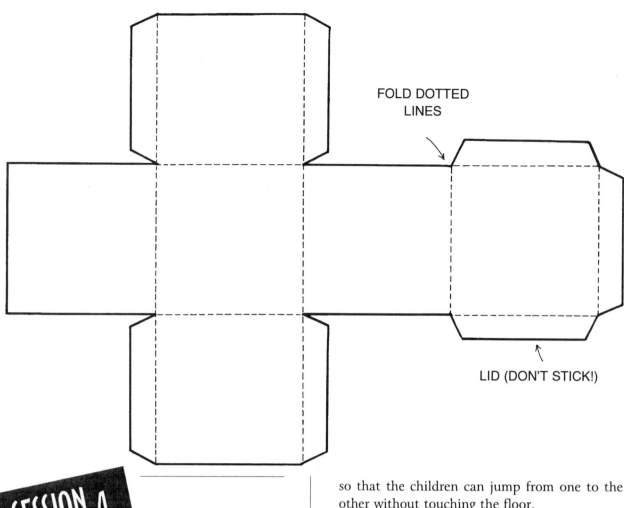

FOLD DOTTED
LINES

LID (DON'T STICK!)

David and Jonathan

1 Samuel 20

Bible Theme
*We need friends to help us
and God uses them*

Way-In Stepping stones

(10 mins)

You will need:
Lots of single sheets of newspaper

Place these sheets at a distance from each other on the floor. They need to be far enough apart so that the children can jump from one to the other without touching the floor.

The floor is shark-infested water and the children have to try and cross from one end of the room to the other without getting eaten by the sharks!

To make it more exciting, you could have one or two 'pirates' who will try to catch them as well – but they too must not get eaten by the sharks!

What did the children use to help them in the game?

Way-In Jelly teaser

(10 mins)

You will need:
Some jelly
2 teaspoons
2 poles or broom handles

Tie two teaspoons to the ends of two long poles or broom handles. The spoons need to be tied firmly, and the poles need to be longer than the children's arms. When the child tries to eat using the spoon and holding the pole at the end, it shouldn't be possible for him to reach his mouth.

Ask for two volunteers who like jelly.

Get them to sit at opposite ends of a table and tell them that you are going to give them a spoon in a moment, and they can eat as much of the jelly as they can using the spoon. The only rule is that they have to hold the pole at the opposite end to the spoon, and they must eat the jelly from the spoon, not with their other hand.

Give the two children the spoons on poles.

The other children can watch their attempts, laugh, and try to suggest how it can be done.

The only way to eat the jelly is for the two children to feed each other!

Let other pairs have a go if they want to.

Draw out of the children the fact that for this game the two volunteers needed each other's help.

 ## Story and discussion

(10 mins)

For the two games the children have played so far, they could not manage on their own, but needed each other's help.

David was in a situation when he needed help. Recall how, in last week's session, Saul was trying to kill David.

Tell the story with as much visual input as possible.

One idea is to draw the pictures from the story for a story line and use this as you tell the story. You can also use it for a game as reinforcement at the end of the story and get the children to put the pictures up again in the correct order, retelling the story as they do so.

Questions for discussion:

1. Who helped David? How did he help him?

2. Was Jonathan a good friend? Why/why not?

3. Discuss the ways that we can be good friends to each other, and any ways in which we have been helped in the past by good friends.

 ## Follow-up 3-legged race

(10 mins)

You will need:
A piece of cloth or scarf per pair of children

Get the children into pairs standing side by side, and tie their inside legs together loosely around the calf area with a scarf or piece of cloth.

Give them time to practise walking or running together, and then have a race.

To do well at this the two friends need to work well together.

Bible verse: Proverbs 17.17
'A friend loves you all the time. A brother is always there to help you.'

Song:
Shalom, my friend

JP 217

Follow-Up
Friendship
bands

(20 mins)

You will need:
Different colours of embroidery silk
Sticky tape
Scissors

Teach the children how to make macramé friendship bands using embroidery silk. They can give the band to a friend.

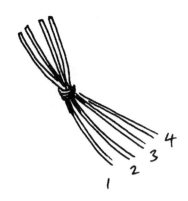

1. Knot one end of your four threads together.

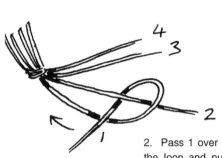

2. Pass 1 over 2, back through the loop and pull tight. Do this twice.

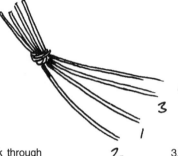

3. 1 and 2 have changed places.

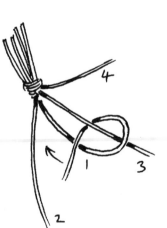

4. Pass 1 over 3 and knot twice as for stage 2.

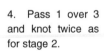

5. 1 and 3 have changed places, so carry on and knot 1 over 4.

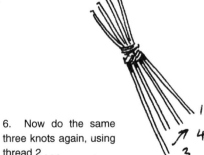

6. Now do the same three knots again, using thread 2 . . .

7. . . . then threads 3 and 4 and so on until you start to weave the band.

46

David spares Saul

1 Samuel 24

Bible Theme
God rewards people who do the right thing

(NB This whole session requires groups of four children to rotate around the various activities. If you are unable to do the cooking, all of the other activities can be done in a large group.)

Way-In
Do the right thing

Big board Game (in groups)

(15 mins)

This is a big board game, in which the children are the counters and take it in turns to move along the board, standing on the squares one by one.

> *You will need:*
> *Cork or carpet tiles, newspaper or card*
> *A large dice*
> *A list of questions (examples are given)*

You need to prepare a big playing board consisting of separate squares. Each square should be big enough for one or two children to stand in. You could use cork or carpet tiles, or a large sheet of card or newspaper for each square.

Some of the squares need to have a large 'Q' written or temporarily stuck on. When the child lands on these squares, he must answer a question correctly in order to move on. The first square should have 'Start' written on it and the last square should have 'Finish'.

The children take it in turns to roll the dice and to move the number of squares on the dice. They have one roll each, unless they land on a 'Q' square. If they land on a 'Q' square, they must answer a question which the leader reads out. If their answer is to 'do the right thing', they can roll the dice again and move on. Emphasise that the children must give an honest answer – what they would really do in that situation, not just the answer that they think is the right one.

The winner is the first one to reach the 'Finish' square.

Examples of questions:

1. A friend at school borrowed your eraser and lost it. Now she wants to borrow a pencil. What do you do?

2. You see two children having a fight at school at playtime. What do you do?

3. You find a pencil on the floor in the hall – what do you do?

After the game is over, discuss how it went. How were they most likely to win?

In this game doing the right thing brings a reward.

Story and discussion

(15 mins)

Talk about the two games that you have played. They both have a connection with the next part of David's life story.

Tell the story with as much visual input as possible.

One idea is to tell the story and then get the children to choose one part of it and mime a 'freeze frame'. The children become the characters from the story and stand absolutely still in the appropriate pose for that scene. Later they do the freeze frame for the rest of the group who have to guess which part of the story it is. To work most effectively, each group must choose a different part of the story to freeze frame.

Questions for discussion:

1. What did David have the opportunity to do to Saul?

2. What did he do? Do you think that he did the right thing?

3. Do you think it was easy for David to do the right thing?

4. Discuss what type of things we find difficult to do but we know are the right things to do.

David will be rewarded by God for doing the right thing. How are we rewarded by God if we do the right things in our everyday lives?

Follow-Up Catch the King!

(in groups)

(15 mins)

You will need:
Lots of old newspapers
Scissors
Rolls of sticky tape
Staplers

Choose one of the group to play Saul.

The others dress Saul up in a newspaper 'robe', using the newspaper, sticky tape and staplers. The robe should be full length and wide at the bottom.

When the robe is completely finished, the children have to try and tear off a little of the bottom of the robe, whilst Saul has his back turned to them and without Saul turning round and catching them.

Follow-Up Cooking rock cakes

(in groups)

(15 mins)

This recipe makes 12 cakes.

You will need:
8oz self raising flour
Pinch of salt
3oz butter or margarine
4oz plain chocolate
3oz castor sugar
1 egg (beaten)
2 tablespoons milk
Sieve
Large mixing bowl
Knife
Large metal spoon
Greased baking tray

Set the oven to 180°C, 350°F or Gas Mark 4.

1. Sift the flour and salt into a large mixing bowl.

2. Add the butter or margarine, cut in pieces and rub into the mixture.

3. Cut the chocolate fairly coarsely and add to the flour along with the sugar.

4. Mix well and stir the beaten egg and milk into the flour.

5. Mix well and then pile the mixture into rough heaps on the greased baking tray.

6. Place in the centre of the preheated oven for 10-15 mins.

Bible verse: Psalm 37.17
'the Lord supports those who do right.'

David is crowned King
2 Samuel 1-5

Bible Theme
God keeps His promises!

Way-In Blindfolded food tasting

(15 mins)

You will need:
Samples of tasty food
Spoons

Keep the samples hidden from the children as they arrive.

The children should get in pairs. Tell them that one of the pair is to be a 'feeder' and the other will be a 'taster'. They can swap around half way through the game. The taster will be blindfolded and has to guess what food they are eating.

Tell the children that you won't give them anything horrid or that they will not like.

After they have finished, discuss the tasting. Who trusted you to keep your promise not to give them anything horrid? Did some trust you more than others? Did they trust you more as time went on? Why?

Story and discussion

(10 mins)

Talk about the game that you have played. What did God promise David right back at the beginning of his life?

Tell the story with as much visual input as possible.

One idea is to 'interview' David (played by another leader). In this way you can bring together all the different experiences of David's life from God's initial promise many years ago, through times of difficulty to the point where David becomes King and realises that God has kept His promise.

Questions for discussion:

1. Did God keep His promise to David?

2. Do you think it was easy for David while he was waiting for God to keep His promise?

3. Discuss the promises that God has made to us. Will He keep them? Is it always easy for us to trust that God will keep His promises?

Follow-Up
This is your life

(15 mins)

You will need:
Coloured card and paper
Scissors
Glue

Make simple objects from the whole of David's life out of paper or card, e.g. a sheep or shepherd's crook, spear, lyre, King Saul, ripped robe, bow and arrow.

You can hide the objects all around the room and get the children to look for them. They must only collect one each.

Or you can just give them one object each, and go on to the next part of the game.

You can go into as much detail as you like trying to put on a version of 'This is your life' for David, such as having a red book, or playing the television theme music. One of the leaders should play the presenter, and you should set up a tape recorder or video recorder with a microphone to record the interviews. Each child should be encouraged to say a sentence (or more, if they can) about the aspect of David's life represented by the object that they have. This is best done in the correct chronological order as far as David's life goes. You might need to have a practice before you actually 'go live' and record it. Try as much as possible to let the children come up with their own words. When you have finished, play the tape or video recording back.

or

Follow-Up
David rap

(15 mins)

This is probably an activity that works best with older children. However, if you want to make up a simple rap yourself for the children to use, then it is also suitable for the 4-6s.

For older children, you could all work together on making up a simple rap using 2 Samuel 7.8-29 or 2 Samuel 23.1-7.

Learn and perform the rap together.

Follow-Up
Making crowns

(20 mins)

You will need:
Coloured card
Feathers
Glitter glue
Sequins
Glue
Stapler

Use the card to make the crowns as shown on the next page.

Older children could design their own hats, using a similar technique.

Bible verse: Psalm 145.13b
'The Lord will keep his promises.'

Song:
Jesus keeps His promises

KP 71

Christmas

For older children discuss the differences. Could they be King David's people? Why not? Was David King for ever? In the Bible, Jesus is described as 'an even greater King than David'. How was Jesus an even greater King than David?

A King like David?
Luke 1.26-38 (& 67-80 for leaders)

Bible Theme
Jesus was to be an even greater King than David

Way-In
The King's people

(10 mins)

You will need:
Large and small mats, or oddments of carpet
Paper
Sellotape
Whistle

The object of this game is to illustrate the fact that King David's kingdom did not have enough room for everyone. David could not be everyone's King. Jesus is a greater King because he has room for everyone.

Way-In
Guess who?

(10 mins)

The children sit in a circle. One child is chosen to go outside the room, whilst the leaders choose the name of a famous person. The child is brought in and has to guess who the famous person is, by asking children or leaders questions to which they must only answer yes or no. This game has most impact if you start off by choosing a King or Queen that they are familiar with (e.g. Queen Elizabeth II, King Henry VIII). The second time around, choose King David. Lastly, choose Jesus.

What had all these people in common? They are all Kings, including Jesus.

Tape the mats or carpet to the floor.

On the small mat write or stick on a piece of paper with the words 'King David'.

On the large one write 'King Jesus'.

Use the small mat only for the first rounds of the game. The children are allowed to run anywhere in the room, but when you blow the whistle, they need to run to the safety of King David's kingdom. Anyone who cannot fit on is chased by the leaders and if caught, is out of the game. Children in King David's kingdom are safe. Play this again until no more children can be caught.

Why is the game difficult? Because King David's kingdom does not have room for everyone.

Now play the same game with the large mat – King Jesus' kingdom. Play as many times as you like or have energy for. It will be almost impossible to catch many children.

Why is this game easier than the previous one? Because King Jesus' kingdom has room for everyone. Jesus is an even greater King than David, because anyone who wants to can belong to him.

Story and discussion

(10 mins)

Talk about the games you have played, which have showed us that Jesus was a King like David, but even greater.

Tell the story with as much visual input as possible. (One idea is to tell this story using puppets.)

Questions for discussion:

1. What did the angel tell Mary?
2. What kind of King was Jesus going to be? How was He different from King David?

Follow-up
A greater King than David

(10 mins)

You will need:
Sheets of coloured paper

4-6s You need five different coloured strips of paper, one colour for each set of two sentences comparing King David with King Jesus. Write the sentences in the box below on the paper strips and hide them around the room.

When the children have found all the pieces of paper they must pair up with the child who has the same colour piece of paper as they have. Then the pairs take it in turns to read out (helped by leaders if appropriate) the sentences comparing King David with King Jesus.

7–10s Prepare the papers by cutting the colours into strips, and use one colour for the sentences about King Jesus and the other colour for those about King David. Write the sentences in the box below on the paper strips and hide them around the room.

When the children have found all the pieces of paper they must find their parallel fact about the other King. When they have paired up correctly, they must take it in turns to read their piece of paper out to the other children. The children will then be able to compare King David and King Jesus.

King David	*King Jesus*
David was King of Israel	*Jesus is King of everyone*
David isn't a King now – he's dead	*Jesus is and always will be King*
Only Israelites were David's people	*Anyone can be Jesus' people*
David saved his people from many enemies	*Jesus saves us from punishment*
David was a man	*Jesus is God*
David loved his people but let them down	*Jesus loves his people and never lets them down*

Follow-up
A 3D
Christmas
card

(20 mins)

You will need:
Template
Pencils
Card (1 x A4 sheet per child)
Coloured paper or card (1/2 x A5 sheets
    per child)
Scissors
Glitter
Glue

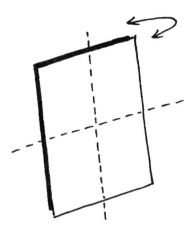

1. Fold A4 sheet of paper across the length and width.

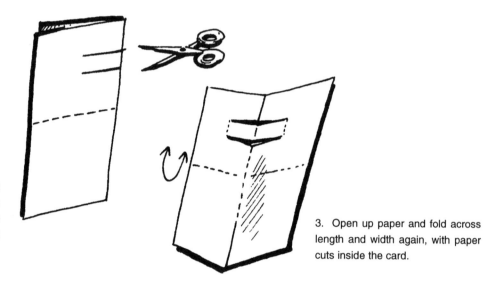

2. Keep paper folded just lengthways. Make two cuts into paper, about 1/4 of the way down the sheet and on the fold.

3. Open up paper and fold across length and width again, with paper cuts inside the card.

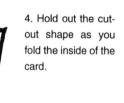

4. Hold out the cut-out shape as you fold the inside of the card.

5. Draw a crown on the other sheet of card and stick inside the card on the pop-out section.

SESSION 2

Getting ready-
Jesus and John

Luke 1.57-80

Bible Theme
God was getting the world ready for Jesus

Way-In
Duck, duck, duck . . . goose!

(10 mins)

The children sit in a circle and one of them is chosen to be 'it'.

This child walks around the outside of the circle, touching every child on the head as he goes, and as he does so saying either 'duck' or 'goose' for each child.

When he says 'goose', the child who is the goose has to get up quickly and chase the child who is 'it' around the circle and back to his place.

If the goose does not catch the child who is 'it' then the goose becomes 'it'.

If the goose does catch the child who is 'it', then 'it' has another go.

Draw out from the children the fact that they all have to be ready to jump up, because they don't know if it's going to be their turn to be a 'goose'. How do they make themselves ready?

Way-In
Ready race

(15 mins)

The children are in teams for this game.

You will need:
A variety of dressing up clothes

Prepare a props box, with clothes appropriate for different job (such as a white coat and stethoscope for a doctor, or a wooden spoon and apron for a cook).

The leader calls out specific jobs, and the children must take it in turns to run up and get ready to do that particular job, by finding and putting on the correct clothes.

This game is all about getting ready, but getting ready appropriately. Ask the children how they got ready to do a particular job.

Way-In
Get ready!

(5 mins)

As the children finish the previous game, prime a leader to come rushing in saying he's just remembered that a very special guest is expected. He makes a big fuss pretending to get the room ready for the very special guest, tidying things away, cleaning up, putting out some food, etc.

He tells the children that they have got to get ready too. How will they do this?

Story and discussion

(10 mins)

Talk about the games that you have played – the need to be ready, to get ready in the right way, and what is the right way to prepare for a very special guest.

Tell the story with as much visual input as possible. (One idea is to use pictures stuck onto a story cube, to show the children as you tell the story.)

Questions for discussion:

1. Why was John the Baptist sent by God ?

2. How were the people to get ready for Jesus, according to John?

Follow-up
Getting ready for Christmas – an advent candle

(20 mins)

You will need:
1 long (12") candle per child
Enamel paint
Rulers
Embroidery needles
Paint brushes

For younger children, you will need to mark the candle at about half inch intervals down its length with a needle, using the ruler to help. Older children can mark their own. You need 25 marks, one for each day of advent.

Paint lines at the marks, and if desired, also paint designs on the candle. Light the candle each day in December and let it burn down to the next line.

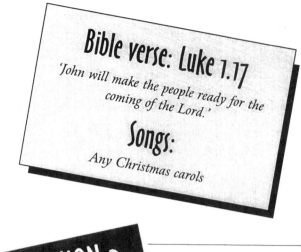

Bible verse: Luke 1.17
'John will make the people ready for the coming of the Lord.'
Songs:
Any Christmas carols

SESSION 3

The birth of Jesus
Matthew 1.18-2.12 & Luke 2.1-18

Bible Theme
Jesus is Emmanuel – God is with us

Way-In
Silhouettes

(15 mins)

You will need:
1 sheet of A3 paper per child
Several angle-poise lamps or spotlights
Pencils
Scissors

Stick the pieces of paper on the wall, and shine the lights on the paper – one light on each piece of paper. Individual children must sit between the lamp and the paper so that a shadow is cast on the paper. A leader should draw around the silhouette (or another child for older groups of children). The paper is then removed and the child cuts out his own silhouette.

When they have all made a silhouette, get the children together and hold up the silhouettes one by one. The children have to guess who each one is.

How could you tell who was who? (They were images of each child i.e. exactly the same as the child). Jesus is exactly the same as God so when we see Jesus, we see God.

 ## Way-In Draw the same

(15 mins)

You will need:
A piece of paper for each child
A pattern (similar to the one shown)
Pencils

Each child needs a pencil and a piece of paper. They must listen carefully and draw exactly what the leader tells them to. Without showing the children the pattern, the leader should look at the pattern and describe it as best they can to the children.

When the leader has finished telling the children what to draw, they must all put their names on the paper and put their pencils down. Then the leader shows the children what their picture should look like. The child who has drawn a diagram which is most similar to the real one gets a prize.

What would have made this activity easier for the children? If they had been shown the original picture it would have been easy. It's easy to know what God is like, because Jesus came to show us.

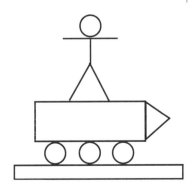

 ## Story and discussion

(15 mins)

Talk about the activities that you have done. Lots of people want to know what God is like. Jesus came to show us what He is like.

Tell the story with as much visual input as possible.

One idea would be to involve all the children in acting the story out, with appropriate costumes.

Questions for discussion:

1. What did Jesus come to show us?

2. How can we know what God is like?

3. Who realised that there was something special about Jesus and that He was more than just a man?

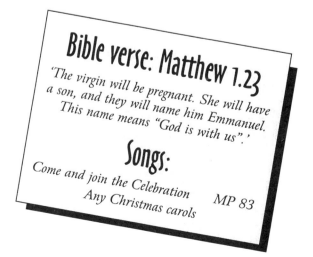

Bible verse: Matthew 1.23

'The virgin will be pregnant. She will have a son, and they will name him Emmanuel. This name means "God is with us".'

Songs:

Come and join the Celebration

Any Christmas carols   MP 83

Follow-up
A 3D star for the tree

(15 mins)

You will need:
Card
Template
Pencils
Scissors
Cotton
Silver and gold glitter
Silver and gold spray paint, powder
 paint, wax crayons or pens

Draw around the template and then cut out two star shapes.

Cut along the line into the centre of the star.

Decorate the stars using the paint or crayons and glitter.

Insert the stars into each other so that they give a 3D effect, and tie a length of cotton to the top so that you can hang the star from the Christmas tree.

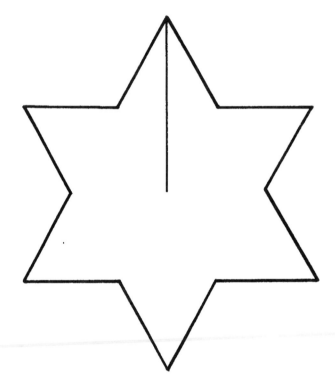

Jesus tells great stories!

SESSION 1

The Lost Coin
Luke 15.8-10

Bible Theme
God is pleased when
He finds one lost person

Way-In
What's
missing?
(5 mins)

You will need:
A tray of about 20 items (all different)

The children close their eyes, and you remove one item from the tray.

They then open their eyes, and the winner is the first one to name the 'lost' item.

Way-In
Missing
piece
(5 mins)

You will need:
Jigsaws (made from an old picture or card)

You need one jigsaw per team. Place these at the opposite end of the room to the team, with one piece missing from each jigsaw.

The children take it in turns to run for one piece of the jigsaw and bring it back to the team.

The rest of team 'build' the jigsaw, whilst it is being collected.

Draw out from the children how they felt at the end of the game when they found one piece was lost.

Way-In
Hunt the
coins
(5 mins)

You will need:
Lots of paper circle 'coins'

Scatter the coins around the room.

The children look for the paper coins. The winner is one who collects the most.

How did the children feel when they spotted a coin and picked it up?

Story and
discussion
(10 mins)

Start by making reference to the two games – the sadness over something that's lost and the rejoicing when it's found.

Tell the story with as much visual input as possible.

One idea might be to tell the story 'in character' of the woman who lost the coin. Dress up appropriately, and use props to give the whole thing authenticity. Bring out the feelings of the woman – sadness when she realises she has lost the coin, determination to find it and joy when it is found.

Questions for discussion:

1. Who is lost to God?

2. In what way are we all lost?

3. How does God feel about us being lost?

4. How does God feel when we are found by Him?

Follow-up
Hunt the coin

(15 mins)

You will need:
A bag of chocolate coins

The children sit in a circle in the centre of the room, and you send one child out. Get another child to hide a chocolate coin in the room.

The child comes back in and tries to find the coin. The children in the circle sing (or clap) louder as the child gets closer to the coin and eventually finds it.

Draw out the parallels of searching for a lost coin and rejoicing when it is found.

Follow-Up
Making coin money boxes
or
Coin necklaces

(20 minutes)

For the money boxes you will need:
A toilet roll middle per child
Card
Yellow sticky paper
Templates for feet, eyes and beak (see illustrations below)
Wool
Scissors
Glue

The children should:

Draw round the templates, cut them out and fold as shown.

Cut a slit (to put the money through) in the toilet roll middle and then cover the roll with the sticky paper.

Stick on the eyes and beak. Stick the feet on the bottom of the toilet roll.

Stick some wool onto the top template and place it in the top of the money box. Do not stick it down as you need to be able to remove the top in order to get the money out again.

For the beads you will need:
   2 cups flour
   Cocktail sticks
   1 cup salt
   Thread or cord
   1 tablespoon cooking oil
   1 cup water
   Powder paint or food colouring
      (mixed with the water)

The children should:

Follow the recipe for each individual colour of dough.

Mix all the ingredients except the water in a bowl. Add the water gradually, until the mixture can be kneaded into a stiff dough.

Make the dough into small balls for beads. Use the cocktail sticks to make holes in the beads and then thread them onto the cord or thread. Leave for a few days to dry out.

Bible verse: Luke 15.10
'There is joy before the angels of God when one sinner changes his heart.'

Songs:
Wide, wide as the ocean
Jesus' love is very wonderful
JP 292
JP 139

SESSION 2

The Great Feast
Luke 14.15-24

Bible Theme
We must say yes to God's invitation if we want to be His friends

Send out invitations to each child for this week's club a few days in advance, or give them to each child at the end of the previous week's club. Make sure that they have RSVP slips to fill in, so that they know that they need to reply to the invitation if they want to come. With 4-6s you will need to make sure that either you or their parent reads the invitation to them.

The first two activities in this session run parallel. Split the group of children in half so that the activities occur simultaneously.

Way-In Cooking

(15 mins)

In small groups, children cook their own cookies. If you do not have the facilities for cooking, they could ice and decorate ready-made cookies or biscuits.

Way-In Table or room decorations

(15 mins)

Again in small groups (at same time as the cooking), they make the table look attractive, with napkins, place names, candles, table decorations and menus.

Alternatively, they could make decorations for the room.

Story and discussion

(10 mins)

Start by making reference to the invitation that they each received to today's party, and also the preparations that they have made for the party. Ask what they felt like when they got the invitation, who has replied to the invitations, and who would like to come. Ask how they would feel if, having made all this effort, nobody came to their party.

Tell the story with as much visual input as possible.

One idea might be to use pictures, including a large (A3) size invitation, while telling the story.

Questions for discussion:

1. What does God invite us to be?

2. What do we need to do to accept his invitation?

Follow-Up

(20 mins)

Have a party!! Eat the cookies and play some party games.

The Persistent Friend

Luke 11.5-13

Bible Theme
God is there to help us if we ask Him!

Way-In Step-up!

(5 mins)

You will need:
Sweets (in their wrapping paper)
Blu-tac

Stick lots of wrapped sweets to the wall, about 6 or 7ft from the floor.

Do not have any chairs, tables, long poles or anything around to help the children.

Ask the children to collect as many of the sweets as they can (and then eat them!)

They'll find it difficult on their own! Watch them carefully to make sure that they do not try anything dangerous.

In fact the only way they can do it (which is safe) is to ask a leader to help them by reaching the sweet for them.

How were the children able to get the sweets? What other types of things do we sometimes need help with? Who can help us?

Way-In
Situations
and solutions

(10 mins)

There are two versions of this game. Use the appropriate one for your age and type of children.

For both you will need:
Large sheets of paper

Write out different 'problems' on the pieces of paper. They should be situations which the children will need some help to 'solve'.

For example, you are making a cake, but cannot reach the top shelf for the sugar. What do you do?

Your cat is very poorly. What do you do?

Try to make the answers to the problems as varied as possible by thinking of the answers that they will probably give. You can do them in picture form if it is more appropriate.

1. Pass the parcel

Put one 'problem' in each layer of the parcel. Also put a treat of some sort in each layer. Play the game, using the rules of 'pass the parcel'. Insist that each child who opens a layer has to find a solution to the 'problem' (by suggesting someone who can help). In return for an answer, the child can eat the treat.

2. Find the solution! *(for readers)*

Write out the different solutions to each of the 'problems' on a piece of paper.

Photocopy the problems and solutions onto coloured paper. Use one colour for each two or three children (the same colour for problems and solutions for each set of children). Cut them up so that each of the problems and solutions are on separate pieces of paper.

Hide all the pieces of paper around the room, and give each group of children (two or three) a different colour to look for. After the children have found all their pieces, they have to put them in pairs – the problem with its solution. Get the children to discuss the solutions and problems and talk about what they would do in the situation.

Story and
discussion

(10 mins)

Talk about the fact that we cannot always do everything by ourselves – even when we grow up! We need help. Jesus told a story about a woman who needed help and got help from a friend. The key is that she asked for help, so she got it.

Tell the story with as much visual input as possible. One idea might be to ask the children to help you out by shouting out various responses that you have planned and practised with them beforehand.

Questions for discussion:

1. Who helps us?

2. What do we need to do for God to help us?

3. Discuss anything that we could ask God for help with. Perhaps you could go round the group actually asking God for these things by praying together.

Follow-up
Need some
help?!

(15 mins)

You will need:
2 cups (filled with water)
Books
Dried peas
Cups and beakers
Long pole
Buckets
Ping-pong balls

Set up various tasks, which the children will find difficult to do on their own:

◆ Carrying 2 cups of water and a book to the other end of the room

◆ Putting as many dried peas as possible from a pile on the floor at one end of the room into a cup at the other end of the room

◆ Carrying a long pole with a bucket on each end the length of the room

◆ Trying to throw as many ping-pong balls as they can into beakers from 2m away – if one misses and lands by the beaker, they can run up and put it in themselves, or leave it and carry on trying with the other balls.

Give them 10 minutes to try doing the tasks on their own, then get the children to do the same tasks in pairs. Is it easier to do the tasks in pairs or on their own?

Bible verse: Luke 11.9

'Continue to ask and God will give to you.'

Songs:

Ask, ask, ask
Father, I place into your hands

JP 11
MP 133

Follow-Up
Talk to God!

(20 mins)

You will need:
Template (below)
Card
Scissors
Glue
Crayons or felt tips

The children can make a 'talking person' from the template below. They can make the person look like themselves, and out of the mouth they can write a sentence such as 'take time to talk to God' or 'God listens when I speak to him'. With non-writers, leaders will need to help the child to write the sentence.

The Two Houses
Matthew 7.24-29

Bible Theme
Hearing and doing what God says is important

Way-In Captain's coming

(5 mins)

Play this so that the children must listen to your commands and obey them. The last person to obey the command each time is out.

Point out that the winner is someone who listens and obeys.

Way-In Taped noises!

(10 mins)

You will need:
A cassette tape
Sheet of paper (per child)
Coloured crayons

Make a tape of familiar sounds, such as pouring a drink, flushing the toilet or striking a match.

Give the child a sheet of paper with pictures of each sound drawn on it.

As the tape is played give the children instructions.

1. Draw a red circle around the object on the sheet which makes this sound.

2. Draw a blue circle around the object which makes this sound, etc.

Mark the answers all together at the end, and discuss what they had to do to get it all right.

Way-In Obstacle course

(10 mins)

You will need:
Chairs
Hoops
Newspapers

Set up an obstacle course consisting of chairs to crawl under, newspaper 'stepping stones' to step on, hoops to pass through, etc.

The children must work in pairs, one blindfolded and the other giving directions so that the blindfolded child can complete the course as successfully as possible. See which pair can complete the course in the shortest time without any mistakes.

Point out that again both listening and doing is important.

Story and discussion

(10 mins)

Make reference to the previous two games and the importance of both listening and doing.

What would have happened in the second game if the blindfolded person had listened but not obeyed?

Tell the story with as much visual input as possible.

One idea might be to use an overhead projector to tell the story as a shadow play. Draw the 'scenery' on several acetates using coloured pens, and make paper wise man, foolish man and houses to lay on the acetates and project as shadows on top of the scenery.

Questions for discussion:
1. What did Jesus say a wise man does?
2. How can we be wise?
3. How can we listen to what Jesus says?
4. What sort of things does Jesus tell us to do?

Follow-up
A jelly baby house or an origami house

(20 mins)

The children listen and obey instructions to tell them how to make the craft items.

For the jelly baby house you will need:
Card
Crayons or felt tips
Jelly babies
Cassette tape

Cut out card houses, using the template on the next page.

Record these instructions on a tape for the children to listen to and follow:

'You have in front of you a jelly baby house. You must decorate the house – put in curtains at the windows and colour the door. You could put a letter box and a number on the door as well. Colour the house, and colour the roof. When you have decorated your house, put the jelly babies in the card 'pockets', looking out of the windows. Your jelly baby house is now finished!'

For the origami house you will need:
Origami paper (cut to about 10cm square)
Red origami paper
Crayons or felt tips

Use these instructions to read out to the children (it would probably help if the leader had a demonstration copy as well):

1. Fold the square piece of paper in half.

2. Unfold it so that there is a fold line running across the paper in the middle.

3. Fold the bottom of the paper up to the fold line in the middle so that the bottom of the paper is touching the fold line.

4. Unfold it again.

5. Fold the top of the paper down to the fold line in the middle so that the top of the paper is touching the fold line.

6. Unfold it again.

7. Now turn the paper around so that all three of the folds are running up and down the piece of paper.

8. Repeat steps 1 to 6.

9. Make cuts as shown on page 68.

10. Fold and stick the house as shown on page 68.

11. Stick the roof onto the top of the house.

12. Decorate the house with windows, curtains, a door, etc.

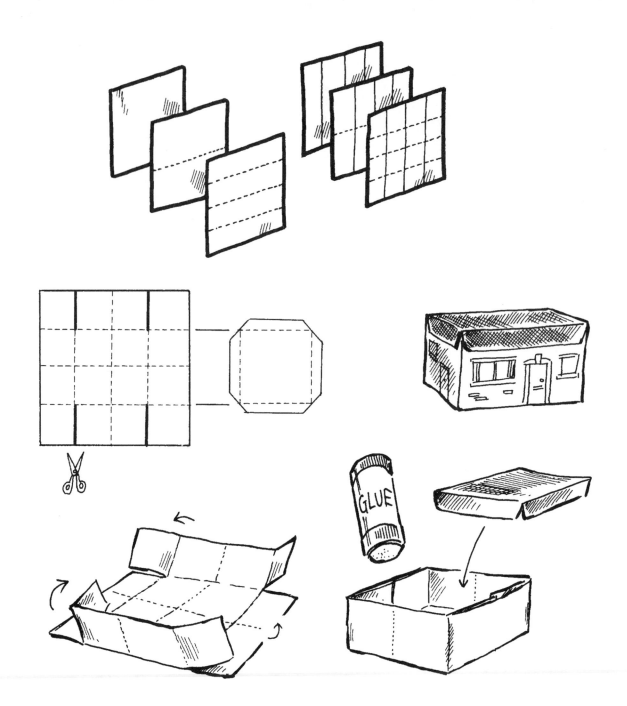

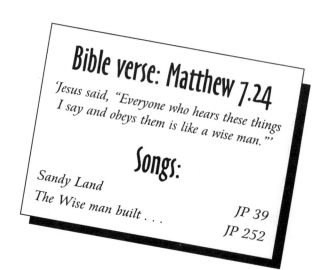

Follow-Up
In the river

(5 mins)

Put two skipping ropes or thick pieces of string across the floor in parallel lines, about 1m apart. In between the ropes is the river, outside the two ropes is the bank.

If you shout 'in the river!' the children must jump in between the two ropes, 'on the banks!' is jumping outside the two ropes. The last one to obey the order is out, as is the person who makes a mistake and jumps into the river (or on the bank) when they're not supposed to!

Bible verse: Matthew 7.24

Jesus said, "Everyone who hears these things I say and obeys them is like a wise man."'

Songs:

Sandy Land
The Wise man built . . .

JP 39
JP 252

68

The Wheat and the Weeds

Matthew 13.24-30 & 36-43

Bible Theme
Good and bad will be separated
at the end of the world

Way-In
Untangle me!

(10 mins)

The children are split into groups of about 6 to 8. One child from each group is sent out. The rest all hold hands, and get tangled up by stepping over each other, going under each other's arms, etc. They must keep hold of each other's hands all the time they are doing this.

The child from outside comes in and tries to untangle the children by giving them instructions. The children must not let go of each others' hands. The winning group is the first group to get the circle back to how it was at the start.

Way-In
Messy string

(10 mins)

You will need:

5 or 6 separate lengths of wool (same colour) for each child, muddled up in a big bundle

5 or 6 separate lengths of two different coloured wools for each child, muddled up in a big bundle

Give each child a bundle of the same colour wool and ask them to untangle it. The first one to separate the pieces of wool from each other is the winner.

Then give each child a bundle of the pieces of two different colours of wool muddled up. See who is the first to untangle them.

Was it quicker to untangle the bundle with two different colours or with the one type of wool? (They should be easier to separate if there are different colours.)

Way-In
Egg heads

(20 mins)

You will need:
2 types of seed
Egg shells (with the top section cracked off) – one per child
1/3 of a toilet roll middle per child
Enamel paint
Paint brushes
Card
Bow tie template (see above)
Scissors
Cotton wool balls
Water

Ensure that the two types of seed look identical.

The children paint a face or a pattern on the egg shell, using enamel paint. They also make and paint a bow tie and half of a toilet roll middle (see diagram).

Then they put a ball of cotton wool inside the shell, dampen it with water and add a few of each type of the seeds (which both look the

same). They put the egg head in the toilet roll middle, and stick the bow tie on the front of the tube, below the egg shell.

Ask the children how to tell the difference between the two types of seed once they are out of the packet. You can only separate them when they have grown and they look different.

Story and discussion

(10 mins)

Start by making reference to the two separating games, and also the seeds used to make the egg heads.

It was easier to separate the wool if it looked different.

When will the seeds look different and therefore be easier to separate? When they have grown.

Tell the story with as much visual input as possible.

One idea might be to draw large pictures to go with the story and make them into a story frieze which you can unfold as you tell the story.

Questions for discussion:

1. What will be separated and when?

2. Who will separate them?

Follow-up Which is which?

(10 mins)

You will need:
Small bar of chocolate
Scraps of newspaper and old cloth
String
3 identical lengths of string each about 5m long

Attach a small bar of chocolate to the end of one piece of string. To the end of the others attach something useless such as an old scrap of newspaper, or dirty torn cloth.

Put the objects about 1m apart and then spread out the lengths of string running from them. Muddle up the lengths of string, separating them out again towards the end of their lengths (see illustration above). The children try to choose the end of the string which will lead to the 'treat' at the other end. They could all have a vote on which one to choose, and then one of them actually finds out whether they are right. If they are, they all get a treat.

The Rich Fool

Luke 12.13-21

Bible Theme
Being truly rich is putting God first

Way-In Shopping mall

(15 mins)

You will need:
Large sheets of paper (A2)
Pencils
Tokens (slips of paper – 20 per child)
Slips of paper

Put the name of a shop on the top of each sheet of paper, and then list the items for sale, and their price (in number of tokens).

Stick the 'shops' to the wall.

Suggestions for the shops, items and prices are:

Games/toys for me		Gift shop		Food shop	
Computer	20	Flowers	2	Chips	1
TV	15	Chocolates	2	Sausages	1
Roller skates	8	Candle	2	Bread	1
Books	2	Glasses	3	Milk	1
Videos	2	Jewellery	3	Steak	2
Bike	10				

You need to have a bank where the children can leave their money if they want to save it instead of spending it.

Each shopkeeper should have some slips of paper to write or draw the item that the children buy on these slips in exchange for the tokens paid.

The children go around with their tokens, deciding what to spend their money on. They have 5 minutes to look and decide, and then another 10 minutes to do their buying. Leaders should be the shopkeepers, take the tokens and give the customers what they have bought.

When time is up, get the children together to talk about their purchases.

What order did they buy things in? Which is the most important thing they bought?

Did they buy the most important thing first? If they had more tokens, what would they have bought? Did anyone bank their tokens? Why?

What were they going to do with the tokens when they got them out of the bank?

Are there things that are important which they could not buy with their tokens?

What is important but cannot be bought with money?

Way-In Wealthy pairs

(15 mins)

This game can be played in small groups of 4 to 5 children.

You will need for each group of children:
Photocopies of the pictures of possessions
(see next page)

Card
Scissors
Glue

Glue the pictures of possessions and other important things in life onto card and cut them out. You need an even number to make pairs.

The cards are all placed face down in the centre of the group of children playing the game.

The aim of the game is for the children to collect as many pairs as they can by turning over two cards at a time. There is a slight twist to the game, however. The pairs are not all worth the same number of points. The more important the picture on the card, the more points that pair is worth. The points for each pair are given on the

5 pts

10 pts

5 pts

2 pts

2 pts

Unless shown, a pair of identical pictures is worth 1 pt. The rest are worth the numbers shown.

sheet, but must be kept a secret from the children until the end of the game.

The child with the most points at the end of the game is the winner.

The children take it in turns to turn over two cards. If they are a matching pair then they keep them and have another go. If they are not, they must turn them back over again. They must try to match the pairs which are the most valuable.

Play the game and then give out the points for the different cards, discussing it if appropriate.

What was a good method for trying to win the game?

Why were some more valuable than others?

Story and discussion

(10 mins)

Talk about the two games you have played.

What do many people think is the most important thing in life? What do they spend a lot of their time trying to do?

The story is about a man who thought that the most important thing in life was to become richer and richer.

Tell the story with as much visual input as possible. One idea might be to play a story game.

Write out the story on different strips of paper. Wrap these chronologically in layers of a parcel with a chocolate coin in each layer as well. Play pass the parcel and read out the story as it unfolds. The children have to decide what to do with the coins they get!

1. What did the man spend his time and energy storing up?

2. Why did Jesus say these were not good things to store up?

3. What does Jesus tell us to concentrate on?

4. Discuss how we can be 'rich towards God'.

Follow-Up The Strongest Tower

(10 mins)

You will need:
Junk modelling equipment (e.g. toilet roll insides, old cereal boxes or old yoghurt pots)
Scissors
Sticky tape
Glue
String

The children have eight minutes to build the biggest and strongest tower that they can, using these materials.

After their time is up, have a good look at each of the towers and decide which you think is the highest. Is it strong as well? Roll a football at the tower to see if it's strong enough. Choose another tower and do the same.

Are any of the towers going to be able to last for ever? Why not?

It is the same with building up treasures like money or toys. They are not as valuable because they will not last for ever. What does last for ever?

Follow-Up Really Rich?

(10 mins)

You will need:
A large piece of paper
Lots of magazines, catalogues, newspapers, etc.

Write the title 'What is being really rich?' onto the piece of paper.

The children stick pictures from the magazines onto the piece of paper to make a large collage. They can also cut up the newspaper headlines to make sentences answering the question 'What is being really rich?', or alternatively you could choose a verse from the Bible story to write at the bottom of the paper to answer the question.

Easter

The Last Supper
Matthew 26.17-30

Bible Theme
Jesus knew what he was going to do

Way-In
Dinner party plates

(10 mins)

You will need:

Plastic or metal plates

Place the plates on the floor (with about one plate between four children). The children must walk around the room without touching the plates. When a leader shouts 'Dinner for four!' the children must grab a plate so that four children are around each plate. Any children who are left over are either out, or must do a forfeit. Play continues in this way with the leader shouting different numbers of dinner parties. On the last round, the leader should shout 'Dinner for twelve!' This provides a suitable link with the story to follow later.

Way-In
Where are you going?

(15 mins)

You will need:
Blindfolds – one per pair of children

For younger children you may prefer to play this game as a group, with one child being blindfolded at a time.

The children get into pairs and one of the pair should be blindfolded.

The other child in the pair has to lead the partner around the room or outside. Then the blindfolded child has to guess where he is.

The children can then swap around so that the other child has a go at being blindfolded.

Did the children know where they were going?

It's hard to know where you are going when you are blindfolded. Jesus knew what was going to happen to him and why.

Way-In
Guess where I'm going

(10 mins)

You will need:
Large strips of paper
4 large place names
2 props or clues

On four large strips of paper write four names of different places that you might visit, such as the swimming pool, a football match or the ice rink. Stick these strips of paper on the four walls of the room.

Questions for discussion:

1. Did Jesus know that he was going to be killed?

2. Why did Jesus give his friends bread and wine?

3. What do Christians do today to remind them of the death of Jesus?

For younger children you might like to draw pictures instead of writing the names of places.

The props you need will depend upon the places you are visiting (e.g. swimsuit and towel for swimming pool; hat, scarf or football sweater for football match, etc).

A leader must put on or use the props, and the children must run to the place name where they think the leader would visit with these props. The last child to reach the right place is out.

What helped them to know where the leader was going?

Story and discussion

(10 mins)

Talk about the games that you have played. Jesus knew what was going to happen to him. He gave his friends a clue so that they would know that he was going to die, and then afterwards remember what he said about his death.

Tell the story with as much visual input as possible.

One idea is to present an 'interview' with one of the disciples at the Last Supper. The disciple, played by a leader, should tell how Jesus seemed to know what was going to happen to Him and was preparing them all for it.

Follow-up Cooking soda bread

(15 mins)

You can either let the children make the dough, or make it yourself beforehand and let the children knead it and shape it.

You will need:
1lb wholewheat flour
2 teaspoons salt
1 teaspoon bicarbonate of soda
1/4 pint soured cream
1/4 pint water

This mixture will make enough for 8-10 children.

1. Mix the flour, salt and bicarbonate of soda.

2. Whisk the soured cream and water together in a jug.

3. Add the whisked mixture to the flour, adding 2 or 3 tablespoons of extra water if it is needed.

4. Knead the dough and then put on a greased baking sheet in a hot oven (220°C, 425°F or gas mark 7) for 30 minutes.

The Crucifixion
Matthew 27.32-56

Bible Theme
Jesus died instead of us,
so we could be forgiven

Way-In Excluded

(10 mins)

The aim of the game is for the children to form small groups of a certain number which you nominate. The size of the group depends upon the number of children you have. You must choose a number that leaves extra children 'left over' and without a group.

For instance, if you have 20 children, choose groups of 3, so that there will be two children left over. When you say 'Go!', the children must get themselves into groups of the number that you have told them. You can play the game as many times as you like, as long as each time there are children left out.

How did it feel to be the left-over ones? Did the other children take any notice of them? Why not? What were they too busy doing?

We are like that with God. We are so busy doing what we want and looking after ourselves that we do not take any notice of him. We ignore him and leave him out of our lives.

Way-In Hare and hounds

(10 mins)

Two children are chosen. One is the hare (being chased) and the other is the hound (chasing). The rest of the children scatter around the room.

The hound must chase and try and catch the hare as he runs in and out of the other players, trying to escape. If the hare thinks he is going to get caught by the hound, he can touch one of the other children and the touched child takes the place of the hare. The game continues in this way. If the hare is caught by the hound then the hare becomes the hound and a new hare is chosen.

How did the hare escape being caught? – by getting someone else to take his place. Jesus took our place so that we could escape the punishment from God that we deserve because we ignore him.

Way-In Substitutes

(15 mins)

You will need:
Layers of newspaper
Sweets
Cassette recorder
Music cassette

Make a 'pass the parcel' with a forfeit and a small sweet in each layer. The forfeits should be quite difficult, so that it is unlikely that the children will be able to do them by themselves.

Play pass the parcel as usual, by passing the wrapped parcel around the circle with the music playing. Explain that there are forfeits and sweets in each layer, and if the parcel stops with you, you can only have the sweet if the forfeit is done. When the music stops, the child holding the parcel unwraps a layer and picks out the forfeit. If the child cannot do the forfeit he can nominate someone else who he thinks will be able to take his place and do the forfeit instead of him. This person (probably a leader) does the forfeit and the child keeps the sweet. Play continues in this way.

Why did the children choose someone else to do the forfeit?

Who got the reward?

Jesus is a bit like the leader who took the child's place. He did what we could not do. He lived a life which followed God all the time and did not ignore Him. He took our place.

But we still get the reward. We'll see how all this happened in the story.

Story and discussion

(10 mins)

Summarise the story from last week. Talk about the games that you have played.

All of us have left God out of our lives, and ignored God. Because of this we deserve to be punished. Jesus took the punishment for us – this is how he did it.

Tell the story with as much visual input as possible.

One idea is to use pictures and a story line upon which you can peg the pictures as you tell the story.

Questions for discussion:

1. What have we done to God?

2. What do we deserve because of this?

3. Why did Jesus die?

For the glaze:
2 tablespoons granulated sugar
2 tablespoons water

1. Stir 1 teaspoon caster sugar into the 1/4 pint warm water, add dried yeast and leave.

2. Sift flour, salt and mixed spice and add sugar, currants and mixed peel.

3. Make a well in the flour mixture and add the now frothy yeast mixture and the milk, beaten egg and melted butter.

4. Mix together well, knead and leave to rise in a lightly oiled plastic bag for an hour.

Follow-up Hot cross buns

(15 mins)

Make the mixture yourself beforehand and get the children to mould the buns, put a cross on the top and glaze them.

This recipe makes 12 hot cross buns.

You will need:
1lb plain flour
1 teaspoon caster sugar
1/4 pint hand-hot water
1 level teaspoon salt
2oz cut mixed peel
2oz butter, melted
2 fl.oz warmed milk
1 level tablespoon dried yeast
1 rounded teaspoon mixed spice
3oz currants
2oz caster sugar
1 egg, beaten

5. Shape into round portions and put crosses on them with either strips of the dough (dampened) or strips of dampened shortcrust pastry. Put in an oven (220°C, 425°F or gas mark 7) and cook for 15 minutes.

6. Make the glaze by melting the sugar in the water over a gentle heat. Brush the buns with the glaze as soon as they come out of the oven to make them sticky.

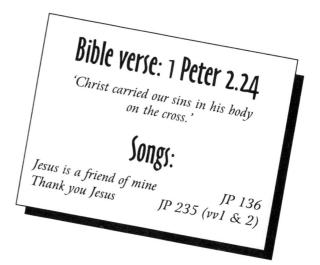

Bible verse: 1 Peter 2.24
'Christ carried our sins in his body on the cross.'

Songs:

Jesus is a friend of mine JP 136
Thank you Jesus JP 235 (vv1 & 2)

The Resurrection
Matthew 28.1-10

Bible Theme
*Jesus is alive now and so can be
a special friend*

Way-In
Dead or alive?

(10 mins)

You will need:
Large sheets of paper
2 pieces of card

Make large pictures of dead and alive objects (see examples on the opposite page). This should include Jesus on the cross, without a corresponding opposite.

Make two large signs saying 'dead' and 'alive' and pin these onto walls on opposite sides of the room.

The children stand in the middle of the room as a leader holds up the pictures one by one. For each one the children must run to the appropriate end of the room, depending upon whether the object is dead or alive. The leader shows the pictures in their pairs, first the 'dead' one and then the 'alive' one. Each time the leader tells them the answer and then the children run back to the centre of the room again. Play continues in this way. End the game with the picture of Jesus – dead and . . . alive?

All the pictures were of things which looked dead but came alive. Jesus was really dead, but did He stay dead for ever?

Way-In
What's in the tomb?

(10 mins)

You will need:
2 large pieces of paper per team
1 dice per team

Pin one sheet of paper per team to the wall, with a large circle outline drawn on it (this is the tomb). Inside the circle draw a few empty, discarded 'grave clothes'.

On another piece of paper per team cut a circle the same size as the large circle outline. Cut the circle into 'brick' shapes, number them 1 to 6, and stick them onto the 'tomb' with Blu-Tak.

Explain that after the soldiers checked that Jesus was really dead they took his body off the cross, and his friends wrapped it in grave clothes and put it in a tomb like a cave, with a massive stone rolled across the entrance. The children are going to get the opportunity now to take the stone away and have a look at Jesus' body in the tomb for themselves. As the stone is so heavy, it has to be removed in sections or parts.

The members of each team take it in turns to roll the dice. When a child rolls a number corresponding to one of the numbers on the brick he runs and removes that 'brick' or part of the stone. If there is no brick corresponding to the number the child has rolled then the dice is passed onto the next child and no part of the stone is removed.

Play continues in this fashion until the whole stone has been removed.

What has happened to Jesus' body?

Story and discussion

(15 mins)

Summarise the story from last week. Talk about the games that you have played.

Tell the story with as much visual input as possible.

One idea is to use a 'trick' birthday cake candle (which relights every time you try to blow it out) as a visual aid during this story. At the start of the story the candle is alight. When you get to the part of the story when Jesus' dead body was put in a tomb, blow out the lighted candle. Carry on with the story and leave the children to notice that the candle has relighted some time later.

Questions for discussion:

1. How did the people know that Jesus was dead?

2. What did some of his friends do to Jesus' body after he had died?

3. What happened to Jesus?

4. Discuss how Jesus being alive affects us here today.

Follow-up
Before
and after

(10 mins)

You will need:
5 colours of paper or card

Before the game a leader should write the following sentences on different strips of paper. Each set of numbered questions should be written on different coloured paper or card.

The children should work in pairs, so you need to write enough for one pair of sentences per pair of children.

Give each pair of children one of the BEFORE strips of paper. Hide all the AFTER strips of paper around the room. Each pair has to look for the corresponding AFTER strip. When all the children have found their strips of paper the pairs of children take it in turns to read out first the BEFORE and then the AFTER strips. (For non-readers the leaders should read out the strips).

BEFORE (Jesus died)	AFTER (Jesus rose again)
1. Punished for our sins	1. Can be forgiven
2. Separated from God by our sins	2. Through Jesus we can be God's friends
3. No hope after death	3. Can go to Jesus when we die
4. No living leader	4. Jesus is alive now
5. No friend to talk to	5. Can talk to Jesus as a friend always
6. Unable to live God's way	6. Have the help of the Holy Spirit so we can live God's way

either be stuck around the middle of the outside of the margarine tub or added to the decoration around the candle (see illustration).

Follow-Up
Easter candle

(15 mins)

You will need:
1 small (10cm x 10cm) cube of flower arranging oasis per child
1 margarine tub per child
A selection of daffodils and greenery
Water
Scissors
Ribbon
Sticky tape
1 small (christingle-type) candle per child

The leaders should cut the oasis to the right size to fit inside the margarine tub. The oasis should also be soaked in water. The children should put the candle in the oasis and decorate around it with the daffodils and greenery. The ribbon can

Bible verse: Matthew 28.6

'The angel said, "Jesus is not here. He has risen from death as he said he would."'

Songs:

Thank You Jesus
Led Like a Lamb

JP 235
SFK 119

Jesus' Friends

SESSION 1

Some fishermen become Jesus' friends

Matthew 4.18-22

Bible Theme
Jesus wants friends to follow Him

(NB If you are working through this series in order you will need to take a head and shoulders photo of each of the children to develop and use next week)

Way-In
Fan the kipper!

(5 mins)

You will need:
Sheets of newspaper
Scissors
Newspapers or magazines

Cut large fish shape 'kippers' out of single sheets of newspaper, one per team or child.

Each child (or team) must use the newspaper to 'fan' the kipper across the floor to the other side of the room. They must try not to touch the kipper with their newspaper, but move the fish by hitting the floor just behind the fish, creating a draught which will push the fish forward.

Way-In
Go fishing

(10 mins)

You will need:
Sheets of coloured paper (4 colours)
4 'nets' (you could buy actual netting,
*   or use the nets oranges are often sold in)*
Colour pencils or crayons

Make lots of small paper fish using the four paper colours.

Staple or glue a larger paper fish onto each of the four nets, a different colour for each net. These nets need to be placed around the room.

To play the game, the children must collect a small paper fish from the leader, put a mark on the back of the fish with their crayon, and then go and place it in the net with the matching colour. When they have done this, they must go and collect another fish, put a mark on it and catch it, and so on. See which child can catch the most fish in the correct nets.

Way-In
Jesus is coming

(10 mins)

Play this version of Captain's Coming, having fishy actions for the children to do when the leader shouts out a particular phrase.

The leader could shout any of the following – 'mend the nets', 'get into the boat', 'row on the lake', 'net over the side', 'haul the net in'. The children are given the appropriate actions for each beforehand. You should include the commands 'Jesus is coming' and 'follow Jesus', again with appropriate actions.

When the leader shouts the command the children must do the correct actions as quickly as possible.

Story and discussion

(10 mins)

Talk about the games that you have just played. These are based on a real story, where Jesus met some real fishermen and wanted them to be his friends.

Tell the story with as much visual input as possible

One idea is to make a massive boat out of large boxes and card, and either tell the story from the boat yourself, or get some of the children to act out the story in the boat as you are telling it.

Questions for discussion:

1. What did Jesus ask the fishermen to do?

2. What did the fishermen do?

3. What does Jesus want his friends to do?

4. How can we know that we are friends of Jesus?

Follow-Up Follow my leader or Follow it

(10 mins)

Either:

Play 'follow my leader', choosing different leaders to have a go.

Bring out the fact that the aim is to follow as closely as possible. We should be following Jesus as closely as possible if we want to be his friends.

Or:

Get the children to sit anywhere on the floor. One child is chosen to be 'it'. This child has to walk around the room and choose someone from the floor by touching them lightly on the head. When touched this child must chase 'it' as he runs, weaving in and out of the other children, eventually arriving back at where the touched child was sitting.

'It' has to try to get back to the chasing child's place before being caught . The chaser has to follow the path of 'it' exactly, or he becomes 'it' immediately. If the chaser catches 'it', then 'it' has to have another go at running away. If 'it' gets away and safely back to his seat without being caught, then the catcher becomes 'it'.

You have to follow the person in front of you exactly to stay in the game. We must follow Jesus if we want to stay his friends.

Follow-Up Fish on a stick or Fish mobile

(15 mins)

For the fish on a stick, you will need:
Card
Felt tips or crayons
Glitter
Pencils
Sellotape
Glue
Lolly sticks or garden canes

The children place their hand onto a piece of card and draw round it. Then they cut out the shape and decorate it using the colouring crayons and glitter. When it is finished stick it on the top of the stick.

For the fish mobile, you will need:
Card
Fish template
Felt tips or crayons
Glitter
Pencils
Cotton
Sellotape
Glue

The children make lots of different fish by drawing around the templates and then colouring and decorating them. They need one large fish and several small ones. Tie up the fish with the cotton as shown opposite.

Bible verse: Matthew 4.22

'At once they left the boat and their father and followed Jesus.'

Songs:

I want to walk with Jesus Christ   SFK 100
I have decided to follow Jesus
JP 98

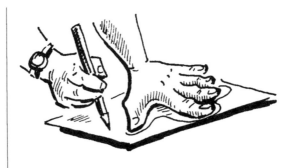

83

A Samaritan woman

John 4.1-30

Bible Theme
*Jesus is a friend who knows us
(and still loves us!)*

(NB If you are doing the craft activity suggested in this session you will need to have taken photos of the children the week before, and had them developed for today. Alternatively, take photos today using instant developing or Polaroid film.)

Way-In Carrying game

(5 mins)

You will need:
Something for each child (or team) to carry on his head, for example a small paperback book.

This can either be played as a team game or individually. The object of the game is to see if the child can cross the room balancing the item on his head and going as fast as he can without dropping the item. No hands allowed!

Way-In Guess who?

(15 mins)

You will need:
*Pencil and paper for each child
Hat or bowl*

Version A (for children who can write)

Give each child a pencil and paper and get them to write down the following:

favourite colour

favourite food

favourite drink

favourite TV programme

They must not write down their name on the paper. They must then fold up their piece of paper and hand it in to the leader.

The leader puts all the paper pieces in a hat or bowl and mixes them up. He then takes one of the pieces of paper out and reads out the list of 'favourites'. The child whose list it is must say nothing. The other children have to try and guess who the author is. When they have guessed correctly the leader takes another slip of paper out of the hat, and so on.

Version B (for children who cannot write)

The children sit in a circle. One child is sent out of the room. While this child is outside, the leader chooses another child, and asks him what his favourite colour, food, drink, and TV programme are (the leader will probably need to write these down).

The child from outside is brought back in, and is told that someone in the room has the following 'favourites'. The leader reads out the list. The child has to guess whose 'favourites' they are. Play continues in this way.

What did you need to be good at this game? Was it easier to guess some people's favourites than other's? Why? What did it depend upon? If you were playing this game with a group of people you had never met before would it be harder or easier? Is there anyone's 'favourites' that it would be very easy to guess?

Way-In Know the Queen?

(15 mins)

You will need:
*A picture of the Queen
(or some other famous person)
A larger marker pen
Large piece of paper*

Stick the picture onto a large piece of paper (A2), leaving lots of room underneath.

Use a large marker pen to write on the piece of paper below the picture. The leader should write the words 'Do you know this person?' directly beneath the picture.

The object of this game is to try to show the children the difference between knowing about a person and really knowing a person as, say, a close friend would.

The children should then be encouraged to tell you all the information they know about the person in the picture. The leader should write the things the children shout out at random underneath the picture.

Most, if not all, of the things the children say will be things they know about the Queen – that she lives in a palace, has some dogs, has four children, etc.

Once they have finished coming up with ideas (or the leader has run out of space!), the leader should ask the children if they think that they know the Queen.

Then the leader should ask some of the following questions:

What is the Queen's favourite colour? favourite food? drink? TV programme?

What makes the Queen sad, angry or happy?

Why don't the children know all the answers to these questions if they know the Queen?

Draw out that although we might know quite a lot about some people, there are very few people who we really know well, as friends. Who knows the children really well? Do even these people know everything about them? Talk about the 'hidden' things in us – what we feel, what we think. Who knows about these things?

 ## Story and discussion

(10 mins)

Talk about the games that you have played – how well we know each other and also if anyone knows us fully.

Tell the story with as much visual input as possible.

One idea is to use puppets as the characters, and use a small model well as the setting.

Questions for discussion:

1. Had Jesus ever met the woman before?

2. What did Jesus know about her?

3. Were all the things that Jesus knew about the woman good things?

4. Did Jesus want to be the woman's friend?

5. What sort of friend do you think Jesus is?

6. Discuss how well Jesus knows us and what type of friend he can be to us.

 ## Follow-Up Jesus knows me and loves me!

(15 mins)

You will need:
1 template per child
The children's photos from the previous week
Glue
Scissors
Felt tips or crayons

The children can cut out their faces from the photos and stick them onto the templates. They can put 'clothes' on themselves by colouring the template using felt tips or crayons. On the back they (or a leader) should write 'Jesus knows me and loves me'.

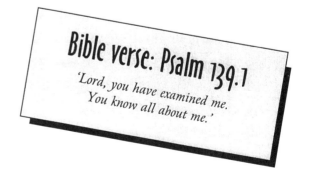
Bible verse: Psalm 139.1
'Lord, you have examined me. You know all about me.'

Matthew
Matthew 9.9-13

Bible Theme
Jesus makes friends with people who know they are bad

Way-In Montage
(10 mins)

You will need:
Old newspapers and magazines
A2 piece of card
Glue
Scissors

Give the children a pile of old newspapers and magazines, a pair of scissors each, and have a large (A2) piece of paper or card and some glue handy. The paper should have a large title – 'People we would choose to be our friends . . .' The children must look through the magazines and newspapers and try to find pictures showing the type of people that they would choose to be their friends. When they have found these pictures, they should stick them on the piece of paper.

After they have finished, talk about the choices they have made, and why. What did they look for in the people they chose? Did they choose people who looked 'good' or people who looked 'bad'? What type of people do you think Jesus would choose to be his friends?

Way-In Target tasks

(15 mins)

You will need:
Ping pong balls
Jam jar
Bowl
Tennis balls
Velcro dart board

Have various tasks set up which are impossible to achieve – 100% successfully anyway! For example: throwing three ping pong balls into a jam jar, throwing three tennis balls into a bowl or hitting the bullseye on a dartboard.

The children play in groups of three and rotate around the different activities. They can have as many goes as they want at each activity, but stress that you are looking for people who never miss the target.

The object of the game is for each child to get all the balls in the jar or bowl and each get a bullseye every time. You could have a big box of chocolates ready for anyone who does hit the target each time. Keep a score of just how many 'bullseyes' and balls in the jar or bowl each child gets.

After everyone has completed the tasks, discuss the results.

Who got 100%? That was the target set. If nobody got 100% then everyone failed to reach the target.

Do not ask for anyone else's scores. It doesn't matter what they all got because they all failed to reach the target. It doesn't matter if they failed by 1 or by 99, they still failed.

It's like that with God and the way we live. God's standards are very high – like having to get 100% in the game. Because none of us have got 100% (we're not all good all of the time, we all do wrong things) then we have all failed God. Some people think that they are better than others and some people might look better than others (like in the picture game), but really we're all the same as far as God is concerned because none of us has reached his target.

Way-In Slipsoaps

(10 mins)

You will need:
Plastic sheeting or dust sheets
A start and finish line
A bar of soap (small enough for the
*   children to get their hands around)*
*   for each team*
A small bucket or bowl of warm water
*   for each team.*

This game can be played outside if weather and space permits.

One child from each team wets his hands and tries to 'shoot' the soap from behind the start line to some way up the course. The rest of his team must try and catch the shot soap. If they successfully do this, then another child from the team takes over from where the soap was caught and tries to shoot it further up the course. If the rest of the team do not catch the soap, then another child has a turn at shooting the soap, and so on until it is caught. Play continues in this way until they have crossed the finish line, and the soap has been caught from the other side.

(NB For younger children, you can play this game without the need to catch the soap each time. The next child takes over from where the soap landed each time.)

What do we use soap for? We all need soap because we get dirty on the outside. We also all get dirty on the inside – that is, doing wrong things (sin) makes us all dirty on the inside.

Story and discussion

(10 mins)

Talk about the games that you have played and about what sort of people we choose to be our friends. What about the target games? Did anyone make the grade and get 100%?

Today's story tells us what happened when Jesus met a group of people who knew that they had failed to reach God's target and were what the Bible calls sinners (people who did wrong things).

Tell the story with as much visual input as possible.

One idea is to get the children to suggest ideas for a tape of sound effects to run alongside the telling of the story, e.g. the sound of rattling money, a group of excited people, eating a meal noises, etc.

Questions for discussion:

1. What type of people did Jesus say that he has come to make friends with?

2. Were the Pharisees 'sinners'?

3. Were they right?

4. What about us?

Follow-up Happy face biscuits

(15 mins)

The tax collectors were happy that Jesus wanted to be their friend. Here the children can make happy face biscuits.

You will need:

Several 'flat' biscuits (e.g. digestive or rich tea) per child

Some coloured icing (you can get tubes of ready-made coloured icing from big supermarkets. The children can squeeze the icing straight from the tube.)

Smarties, silver balls, sugar strands, currants, etc. to decorate the biscuits.

The children can decorate their biscuits as they want.

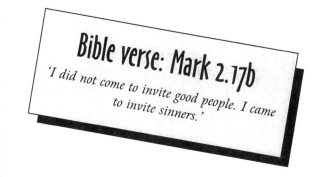

Bible verse: Mark 2.17b
'I did not come to invite good people. I came to invite sinners.'

SESSION 4

Zacchaeus

Luke 19.1-10

Bible Theme
Jesus is a friend who can help you change

Way-In
Cheat

(10 mins)

You will need:
A bag of dried peas
1 straw per child
1 yoghurt pot per team (or per child if playing individually)

The children can play this in teams or individually.

The peas should be on plates at the opposite end of the room from the yoghurt pots.

The children must collect as many peas as they can by sucking them onto the end of the straw and carrying them (on the end of the straw) to the yoghurt pots at the other end of the room.

If they drop the pea on the way between the plate and the pot they must leave it on the ground and collect another one from the plate.

Leaders must turn a blind eye to anyone who cheats by breaking the rules.

After the game is over, ask if anyone was tempted to break the rules. Did anyone actually cheat? See if they will confess to you. If you have seen anyone cheat during the game, say that you actually saw some children breaking the rules – don't mention their names, though. Wait for any more confessions(!) and then make a general comment about how we all break rules all the time, such as school rules, parents' rules and God's rules.

Story and discussion

(10 mins)

Talk about the game that you have played.

Jesus met a man who was a cheat. He became Jesus' friend and something amazing happened to him.

Tell the story with as much visual input as possible.

One idea is to get both children and leaders to act this out. You will need to have a leader to be the narrator. Have the children as the crowd and ask one small child or a leader to be Zacchaeus, and a leader to be Jesus. If it is summer and you have access to a large tree, it would be fun to actually have Zacchaeus climb the tree and to act the whole thing out outside.

Questions for discussion:

1. Why wasn't Zacchaeus a good man?

2. How did he feel when Jesus wanted to become his friend?

3. What happened to Zacchaeus when Jesus became his friend?

4. Discuss what Jesus can do for us if we are his friends.

Follow-up
All Change

(15 mins)

You will need:
A large soft ball

One child is the bowler. All the other children are skittles.

The 'skittles' should stand in a row facing the wall at one end of the room.

The bowler stands at the other end of the room and bowls (rolls) the ball. The aim is to try and hit the skittles below the knee. If a skittle is hit, he must turn around and face the other way.

The bowler has to try and turn round all the skittles with the least number of bowls possible.

To shorten this game play it in teams (if you have more than 10 children), or have a limited number of bowls per bowler and see who can turn the most skittles around.

The purpose of this game was to turn the skittles around. Zacchaeus needed turning around from his cheating. We need Jesus' help too when we break God's rules.

Follow-up Runaround

(15 mins)

You will need:
4 large sheets (A1) of card or
*   newspaper*
A list of questions
A whistle

Label two sheets of paper A and two sheets B.

Prepare a list of questions with different options (A or B) for answers. Examples of the type of questions you can use are given in the next column.

The leader asks the question and then gives the two options for the answer – A or B. The children then have ten seconds to decide which answer they would give. Then they have to run and stand on that piece of paper.

After ten seconds the leader blows a whistle. The children are then given another ten seconds to change their mind if they want to. If they want to change their minds they must run to one of the other pieces of paper.

After everyone has finally decided what answer to give the leader gives the extra piece of information. The children are then given another ten seconds to see if they want to change their minds again, taking into account the extra piece of information they have just been given.

All those who made the wrong decision are out. The rest of the children play again with a different question. Play continues in this way.

Examples of questions:

1. You can choose what to have for lunch on bank holiday Monday. You can choose:

   A – to get a McDonalds

   B – to get fish and chips from the chippy

   extra information: it is a bank holiday and not all the shops will be open.

   right answer: you have to choose answer A because the chippy is closed, so if you chose answer B, you are out.

2. Where would you like to go on holiday? You can go:

   A – camping to Wales

   B – to Butlins

   extra information: the weather forecast is for rain and gale force winds the week you are planning to go.

   right answer: you would be better off choosing answer B, otherwise you and your tent will be washed away!

Draw out the fact that in this game the children needed to change their minds when they heard the extra information in order to make a wise decision. This is a little like Zacchaeus who knew he needed to change when he met Jesus. When Zacchaeus met Jesus he realised he wanted to change, and he needed Jesus to help him change.

Follow-Up Fimo figures

(10 mins)

You will need:

A variety of colours of 'Fimo' modelling material

Either badge pins or magnets to stick on the back (you can usually get these from the place where you purchase the Fimo)

Superglue

Zacchaeus was a little man – get the children to make simple little figures with the Fimo. Then follow the instructions to harden in the oven, and stick the badge pin or magnet on the back with superglue.

Song:
Zacchaeus was a very little man   JP 300

A man through the roof !

Mark 2.1-12

Bible Theme
Jesus is a friend who heals and forgives

Way-In Different ability race

(10 mins)

You will need:
1 tennis ball per team
1 bucket or bowl per team

The teams should sit at the opposite end of the room to their buckets and balls.

Each of the team members should be told what part of their body they cannot use in this game. For example, one child cannot use a left leg, another cannot use a right leg, another their eyes, another a left arm, etc. Have the same number and type of disabilities in each team. The team members are to take it in turns to run to the other end of the room, pick up the tennis ball and throw it into the bucket from a specified distance away. If the child misses he must continue trying until he is successful. The rest of the team can help by shouting out directions, but may not help in any other way. The winning team is the first to have all their team successfully throw the ball into the bucket.

What made this game difficult? Did some team members find it more difficult than others? Why? What if you really could not use that part of your body?

Way-In Handicap pass the doughnut

(10 mins)

You will need:
1 doughnut per team

The game can be played in teams. Alternatively play all together against the clock – have a few goes to find your best time.

The children all need to sit on chairs in a line, as close to each other as possible.

Nominate a couple of people in each team (fairly near each end) to be the two who can use their arms and legs. The other children are to pretend that they cannot use their legs or arms at all, and so must remain seated at all times and not use their arms.

The object of the game is to pass the doughnut down the line from one end to the other, passing from round one child's nose to round the next child's nose. If the doughnut is dropped on the way, it must go back to the start again (but remember the disabilities!).

How did the teams get the doughnut back to the beginning if they dropped it? They needed the help of the two people who could use their arms and legs.

Way-In Jigsaw race

(10 mins)

You will need:
Whole page pictures of people – you need one for each team or child. Cut them up into five pieces, like a jigsaw, but cutting straight sides.

Each child or team also needs a dice.

The children take it in turns to shake the dice. When a six is thrown, the child runs up to the pile of jigsaw pieces and collects one. Play continues in this way until all five pieces have been collected and the person put together so that he is whole again.

The children were making the people whole again. Do people really need making whole again? Who does?

Story and discussion

(10 mins)

Talk about the games that you have played. A man who was paralysed and could not walk needed Jesus' help. But he could not get to Jesus. Why not? Because he couldn't walk. Listen to see what happened to him.

Tell the story with as much visual input as possible. One idea is to have different hats for the different characters in the story, and tell the story wearing the hats at the appropriate time.

Questions for discussion:

1. What did the man need Jesus to do for him?

2. What greater need did Jesus know that the man had?

3. Discuss what our needs are and what we want Jesus to do for us. Also discuss what we think Jesus thinks our needs are.

Follow-Up Soap sculpture

(20 mins)

Having our sins forgiven is a bit like being 'clean' on the inside. Here's a craft activity using something which makes us clean on the outside! Our soap sculpture can remind us of the need to be forgiven by Jesus and be clean on the inside too!

You will need:
2 cups soap flakes (per 2 children)
1/2 cup of hot water (per 2 children)
Powder paint for colouring
Electric mixer
Aluminium foil
*Coloured cocktail sticks, straws,
    small buttons, etc. for decorating
    the sculptures*

A leader will need to prepare the mixture a few minutes (no more) before it is to be used, by adding the hot water to the soap flakes and paint, and beating with a mixer until it is stiff. Have some mixture without paint for those who might want to make a soap sculpture they can actually use.

Children need to dip their hands into warm water before moulding with the mixture.

They should mould it on aluminium foil – this makes it easy to move after it is set, and during moulding. If the children want to use their models as soap then they must use the mixture without paint, and not add any coloured decorations.

Bible verse: 1 John 2.2
'Jesus is the way our sins are taken away.'

93

SESSION 6

Peter

Matthew 14.22-33

Bible Theme
Jesus is a friend we can trust

Way-In Blindfold obstacle course

(15 mins)

You will need:

Set up an obstacle course beforehand. You could have 'stepping stones' made out of newspaper, tables to crawl under, chairs to go around, benches to walk on, etc.

Get a leader to show all the children how to complete the obstacle course, and then tell the children that they're going to get into pairs to do the course. One of the children will be a guide, and the other blindfolded. Let the children form pairs.

The pairs of children take it in turns for the blindfolded child to try and complete the obstacle course, being guided through it by the constant directions shouted out by the guide. The guide can hold the blindfolded child's hand if that will help them, although it is better if possible for the blindfolded child to complete the course unaided, just following the directions given. The children can swap round and do the course again.

Did the blindfolded children find it easy? Did they trust their guides? How did they choose who to be their guide? Would they have trusted anyone to guide them?

Way-In Boiled egg bowling

(15 mins)

You will need:

Several eggs hard boiled and then put back in the egg box

Dust sheets or polythene sheets on the floor if you're playing indoors.

The children need to do this game in pairs – volunteers only!

The first pair need to stand close together. Tell the children that although the eggs look as if you've just bought them, you really have hard-boiled them all.

The pair of children are going to use an egg as a ball and throw it to each other.

They must trust that you are telling the truth about the eggs being hard-boiled, or they'll get very messy.

When one of the pair catches the egg, the other child takes one step back, so the pair are getting further apart all the time. This means that catching it will become harder and harder.

What did you need to be able to play this game? Were you right to have trusted the leaders' promise that the eggs were hard-boiled?

Story and discussion

(10 mins)

Talk about the games that you have played and how important it was to trust the person working with you in the games. One of Jesus' friends needed to trust Jesus in the story today.

Tell the story with as much visual input as possible. One idea is to make a story frieze by joining several pictures from the story together and revealing them one by one as the story progresses.

Questions for discussion:

1. What did Peter need to do in order to keep on the water?

2. Who helped Peter to walk on the water?

3. Discuss things that we need help with or things in which we need to trust Jesus. What sort of things can we trust Jesus with?

Follow-Up Oil paint marbling

(20 mins)

You will need:

A washing-up bowl (or several) half full of cold water

A selection of oil-based paints of different colours (which will need thinning so that they are of liquid consistency)

A4 sheets of paper

The children choose 2 or 3 different colours, and add a few drops of each colour to the surface of the water. They can mix the colours by blowing gently on the water, or by stirring the water gently with a stick.

Then a piece of paper is placed gently on the surface of the water for a few seconds, before being removed carefully and left somewhere for a while to dry.

(Hint: by using a template as shown below, the children can design and make their own writing paper.)

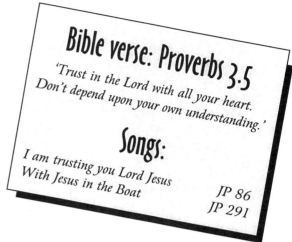

Bible verse: Proverbs 3.5

'Trust in the Lord with all your heart. Don't depend upon your own understanding.'

Songs:

I am trusting you Lord Jesus   JP 86
With Jesus in the Boat   JP 291

SESSION 7

Mary and Martha
Luke 10.38-42

Bible Theme
Jesus is a friend who we should listen to

Way-In Get busy!

(10 mins)

You will need:
Plastic sheeting or newspapers (if playing inside)
Bowls of warm washing up water
'Dirty' plastic plates
Drying up towels

Put a large plastic sheet or lots of newspapers on the floor in case of any accidents!

Have several bowls of warm washing up water (with lots of bubbles). If you are playing as a team game, you need one bowl per team.

You also need plenty of dirty plastic plates, a washing cloth or brush and a drying up towel.

The children must run to the washing up bowl and wash a plate in the soapy water. Then the next child runs to the bowl and either dries the washed up plate or washes another dirty one. Play continues in this way, until all the dirty plates have been washed and dried.

Way-In Chinese whispers

(10 mins)

Get the children sitting in a line (or two lines if you want to play this as a team game). The leader passes a message to the first child in the line by whispering in his ear. The children must pass the message on by whispering down the line. The last child must say out loud the message they heard.

Send messages appropriate to the teaching point e.g. 'Are you good at listening?' 'Would you rather be listening or washing up the pots?' 'Who do you listen to most?' 'Are teachers worth listening to?'.

Discuss how good at listening the children were. Was it easy? Did they have to concentrate?

Way-In Sending messages

(10 mins)

You will need:
Pencils and paper
Prepared messages

The children need to be in pairs for this game.

The children should be sitting at opposite sides of the room in two lines, each pair facing each other.

If the children are readers/writers, one half of the pairs needs a pencil and a piece of paper.

Give one of each pair (the child without the pencil and paper) a short sentence to remember. All the sentences should be the same length, and all should be different.

At the given signal the children with the sentences have to shout them out as loudly as they can to their partner sitting opposite them on the other side of the room.

The partner must write it down (if using pencil and paper) or remember it, and then repeat it back to the first child to make sure it's correct.

After a few minutes the game is stopped and you can see how many of the pairs correctly communicated the message by asking the receiver of the message to tell you what it is.

Why was this game hard? – lots of voices made it hard to listen properly.

What did the receiver have to make sure he was doing? – listening to the right voice. It's important for us to listen to the right voice – which people's voices is it good for us to listen to?

 # Story and discussion

(10 mins)

Talk about the last two games that you have played, how important it was to listen to the person working with you in the games. When is it hard for us to listen? – when there are other distractions like others talking, other things to do, etc. One of Jesus' friends needed to listen to Jesus in the story today.

Tell the story with as much visual input as possible. One idea is to have the story recorded on a tape recorder and get the leaders to mime out the story as the tape recording is played. This links in well with the theme of listening.

Questions for discussion:

1. What did Martha think was important?

2. Who had chosen the most important thing to do and what was it?

3. Discuss ways in which we can listen to Jesus. How often do we do it? How often should we do it? How important is it for us to listen to Jesus?

 # Follow-Up Make a film strip

(20 mins)

You will need:
Clear OHP acetates
*   (1 per child)*
OHP pens (4 colours or more)
Card frame (see illustration below)

The children make their own illustrations on strips of OHP acetate cut to the appropriate size, and colour in their pictures. Make the frame out of card.

If you've time some of them could 'show' the film using a torch to project the film and narrating the story themselves.

The Ten Lepers
Luke 17:11-19

Bible Theme
Jesus is a friend who we should thank
for what He gives us

Way-In Role-plays

(15 mins)

These role-plays are designed to communicate the same point. It's good to say thank you to people who do things for us, but we don't always do it.

Get the children into groups of four or five. You need one leader per group, who needs to lead the role-play and is already primed as to the scene, and what part (s)he should play.

The groups should perform their role-play to the rest of the group. No practice is needed. In fact, it works better if you do not practice first. Ask all the children to watch and listen carefully. They must then try to find the common thing between all the plays.

Group A

The leader is a Mum, and the children are her children. The leader should ask the children to do various tasks for her, such as washing up or tidying their rooms. When (or if!) they do them, the leader should not say thank you to them, or offer them any other words of encouragement.

Group B

The leader is a teacher. The children are the pupils. The teacher hands out some work and expects the pupils to get on with it. The teacher realises that you need scissors and a pencil. Not everyone has them. The teacher sends someone to get them and hand them out. The teacher should not thank the pupil for getting them and handing them out. (Notice how many of the other pupils say 'thank you' as well.)

Group C

The two leaders are best friends. They have put on a tea party for their guests (the children). As the guests arrive their coats are taken and the food served. One leader should be reminding the guests who are not saying thank you all the time to say thank you. But when the other leader does something for this leader, he does not say thank you.

See if the children get the common link – that we don't always remember to say thank you all the time.

Draw out how the children felt when the leaders did not say thank you to them in the plays. How do people feel in real life when we forget to say thank you?

Who should we often say thank you to?

Way-In Magical handshakes

(10 mins)

You will need:
2 bars of chocolate

Give two people (responsible children or leaders) a bar of chocolate. They are to hide it (in a pocket or up a sleeve) somewhere on their person so that nobody knows that they have it.

The children and leaders are to circulate around the room, shaking hands with each other. They are told that one handshake may turn out to be 'magical' as there are two people with chocolate bars, and if you are the fourth person who shakes hands with one of them you might get a prize.

The two people with the chocolate bar have to give it to the fourth child who shakes their hand. When they have given the chocolate bar away, the child who receives it must say thank you, or the person who gave it must take it back again. If they have to take it back again they must start from the beginning and try the fourth person again when they come around. Play continues in this way until both the chocolate bars have been gratefully received.

The children only received the chocolate bar if they said thank you for it.

Story and discussion

(10 mins)

Talk about the games that you have played – how important it was to say thank you. Tell the story with as much visual input as possible. One idea is to make up a choral poem or rap from the story, with a chorus that talks about the importance of saying 'thank you'. Either make it up in advance and chant it together, or get the children to make it up together and then chant it.

Questions for discussion:

1. Who had something to thank Jesus for in the story?

2. How many lepers actually did go back and say thank you to Jesus?

3. How do you think Jesus felt when the other nine lepers did not go back and thank him?

4. Have we got things to thank Jesus for? If so, what? Discuss these things and then perhaps spend time with each child thanking Jesus for something, if it seems appropriate.

Follow-Up Alleluia, Amen

(10 mins)

All the children sit in a circle. One child is chosen to stand in the middle. This child points to any player in the circle and says one of the following:

1.	*Alleluia!*	*player's response:*	*Amen!*
2.	*Amen!*		*Alleluia!*
3.	*Allelu-Amen!*		*Amen-Allelu!*
4.	*Amen-Allelu!*		*Allelu-Amen!*

With younger children you might like to use only two responses.

The player must answer immediately with the right response. If it is either incorrect, or not immediate then the chosen player becomes 'it' in the middle. If the chosen player answers correctly, then the child in the middle must point to another player and repeat the procedure. Play continues like this.

Tell the children that 'Alleluia' means 'Praise the Lord' and 'Amen' means 'I agree'.

Don't forget to thank God for what he's done for you!

Follow-Up Finger puppets

(15 mins)

You will need:
Templates traced
*   or photocopied onto white card*
Colouring crayons or felt tips
Scissors
Sticky tape

The children cut out the templates and colour them in, stick them to make finger puppets.

Bible verse: Psalm 107.1
'Thank the Lord because He is good.'

Songs:
Thank You
O, O, O how good is the Lord   JP 230
                                JP 180

Lazarus

John 11.1-44

Bible Theme
Jesus gives us everlasting life

(If you are doing the craft activity at the end of this session, you might want to paint the pots at the start of the session so that they are dry and ready to be used at the end of the session.)

Way-In Mummy game

(10 mins)

You will need:
plenty of toilet rolls

Split the children into groups of four. One of the children should be nominated to be the 'mummy' – to be wrapped in toilet roll from head to toe. He must stand completely still in the centre of the group.

Each group is given 3 rolls of toilet paper and the other 3 children in the group should set about wrapping the child in the toilet paper so that none of the child is visible (but leaving space for the nose!) when they've finished. (Save the toilet paper to be used again.)

Explain that in the times the Bible was written, this is what people did to a person who had died, before being put in a tomb.

Way-In Dead lions

(10 mins)

The children should lie on the floor in any position that is comfortable. They are to pretend to be dead – to be as still as possible and try not to move at all.

If the leaders spot any of the children moving then they are out.

Story and discussion

(10 mins)

Talk about the games that you have played. Two of Jesus' friends needed his help because their brother had died.

Tell the story with as much visual input as possible. One idea would be to have a surprise message from one of the sisters saying that her brother is dying and could Jesus come quickly. You could have a second message later saying that he's already dead, so there's no point in Jesus coming.

Questions for discussion:

1. What did Jesus do for Lazarus?

2. What did Jesus promise after that to anyone who believed in him?

Follow-up Painting pots and planting bulbs

(30 mins)

You will need:

Water

1 small plastic plant pot per child (diameter about 5")

1 bulb per child

Some potting compost

Enamel paint

Paint brushes

Masking tape

The children need to paint their pot with enamel paints. For younger children, you might want to stick masking tape around the pot beforehand so that the children find it easier to decorate (see illustration). Older children can stick the masking tape on themselves if they want to use it. The children can paint any design on the pots and then leave them somewhere safe to dry.

Make sure the paint is dry before planting the bulb. The children put some potting compost in the pot about a third up the pot. Then they put in the bulb and add more compost almost to the top of the pot, firming down well with their fingers. Finally the children should water the bulb and take it home (watering when dry) and wait for new life to appear.